TWAYNE'S WORLD AUTHORS SERIES

A Survey of the World's Literature

Sylvia E. Bowman, Indiana University
GENERAL EDITOR

GERMANY

Ulrich Weisstein, Indiana University
EDITOR

Theodor Storm

(TWAS 252)

TWAYNE'S WORLD AUTHORS SERIES (TWAS)

The purpose of TWAS is to survey the major writers —novelists, dramatists, historians, poets, philosophers, and critics—of the nations of the world. Among the national literatures covered are those of Australia, Canada, China, Eastern Europe, France, Germany, Greece, India, Italy, Japan, Latin America, the Netherlands, New Zealand, Poland, Russia, Scandinavia, Spain, and the African nations, as well as Hebrew, Yiddish, and Latin Classical literatures. This survey is complemented by Twayne's United States Authors Series and English Authors Series.

The intent of each volume in these series is to present a critical-analytical study of the works of the writer; to include biographical and historical material that may be necessary for understanding, appreciation, and critical appraisal of the writer; and to present all material in clear, concise English—but not to vitiate the scholarly content of the work by doing so.

Theodor Storm

By A. TILO ALT

Duke University

Twayne Publishers, Inc. :: New York

Dem Andenken meines Vaters gewidmet

Preface

The aims of this book were twofold: first, and in keeping with the stated purpose of the series, to provide an overview and an introduction to Theodor Storm, and, second, to present a consistent point of view concerning the entire work of Theodor Storm. In view of Storm's lifelong struggle with a tragic view of the world within the limits of a realistic style and the art of the novella, the aim of this study was to shed light on this struggle by providing a typology of Storm's prose and poetry. Therefore, structural criteria largely determined the principle of selection. The eight novellas discussed were chosen on the grounds that they provided various types of framed novellas, narrative perspectives, and techniques representative of Storm's prose as a whole. Richard Brinkmann's study *Wirklichkeit und Illusion* (Tübingen: Max Niemeyer, 1957) provided the categories of "subjective" and "objective" presentation, of "reality" and "illusion." These terms were applied to Storm's prose and to his lyrical poetry whenever possible. (For the sake of convenience, a summary of Brinkmann's theories is provided under "Notes and References.")

The hermetic form of the novella, as well as the intimate forms of the lyric, were the means for Storm to come to terms with a reality which he viewed alternately as tragic and meaningless. In his lyric oeuvre as well as in his prose, Storm sought to create a tragic emotion in his reader, the dialectic of which, as this study attempts to prove, finds its synthesis in Storm's last and most important work, *Der Schimmelreiter*. Through its main character, Hauke Haien, Storm created the myth and legend of the modern tragic hero whose life and death lend meaning to a prosaic and confining reality.

For the chapter on the lyric poetry, the same principle of selection was followed as for the prose, although the risk of having made an unrepresentative choice is obviously much greater, given a total of some three hundred poems written by Storm.

Finally, the translations of the poems quoted in the study require comment. In order to preserve the meaning and flavor of Storm's poetry, a compromise had to be struck between a creative and a literal translation. Therefore, the verses quoted in the text are rendered in prose translation as well as in the original. In this way, it is hoped, the reader will be able to turn to the German originals for prosodic and other points.

Thanks are due the Faculty Grants Committee of Mount Holyoke College and the Research Council of Duke University for financial support, enabling the author to travel to the Storm Archives in Kiel and Husum, Germany. Thanks are also due Mrs. Irma Fischer and Mrs. Frieda Wetzenstein, both librarians at the State Library in Kiel, Professor Olaf Klose, former director of the Kiel Library, Dr. Karl-Ernst Laage of the archives in Husum, and Professor Ulrich Weisstein, the editor of Twayne World Authors Series. Their help was essential to the writing of this monograph. Finally, a word of gratitude to Miss Betty Steedly who typed the greater part of the manuscript.

The abbreviations used in the notes are as follows:
K = *Theodor Storm, Sämtliche Werke.* Ed. Albert Köster, 8 vols.
G = *Theodor Storm, Sämtliche Werke.* Ed. Peter Goldammer, 4 vols.

ARTHUR TILO ALT

Duke University

Contents

Contents

Chronology

1817   Theodor Storm born on September 14 in Husum, Duchy of Schleswig, a Danish citizen.

1835   Attends the high school in Lübeck, meets Emanuel Geibel; friendship with Hegel's disciple, Ferdinand Röse.

1836   First encounter with Bertha von Buchan.

1837   Enters Law School at the University of Kiel.

1838   Continues studies at the University of Berlin; takes a trip to Dresden.

1839   Returns to Kiel; friendship with the brothers Theodor and Tycho Mommsen.

1842   Receives law degree at Kiel; Bertha von Buchan refuses his hand in marriage.

1843   First publication of his poems in *Liederbuch dreier Freunde* by Storm and the Mommsen brothers; begins to practice law in Husum.

1844   Engaged to his cousin, Constanze Esmarch.

1846   Marriage.

1848   Collaborates with Theodor Mommsen in the prorevolutionary *Schleswig-Holsteinische Zeitung*.

1849   *Immensee*.

1852   *Gedichte* (first edition); meets Theodor Fontane in Berlin.

1853   December: exile to Potsdam and an unpaid position at the district court there; joins the literary society "Tunnel über der Spree."

1854   Meets the Romantic poet Joseph von Eichendorff in Berlin.

1855   Visit with Eduard Mörike in Stuttgart.

1856   September: accepts position as district judge in the Prussian town of Heiligenstadt.

1859   *Auf dem Staatshof*; edition of his first lyrical anthology, *Deutsche Liebeslieder seit J. Chr. Günther*.

1862   *Im Schloss; Am Kamin; Unter dem Tannenbaum*.

1863   *Auf der Universität; Abseits.*

1864   March: return to Husum after its liberation from Danish rule; becomes district judge and chief of police; *Die Regentrude; Bulemanns Haus.*

1865   May 20: Constanze dies; September: visit with the Russian writer Ivan Turgenev in Baden-Baden. *Der Spiegel des Cyprianus.*

1866   June 13: marries Dorothea Jensen, called Do by him and his children.

1867   Abolition of his office in the wake of Prussian reforms; becomes a lower court judge.

1868   First edition of his collected works: *Sämtliche Werke* in six volumes (Georg Westermann).

1870   Storm's second anthology of lyrical poetry, *Hausbuch aus deutschen Dichtern seit Claudius.*

1872   *Draussen im Heidedorf;* trip to southern Germany and Austria; visit with Paul Heyse in Munich.

1876   *Aquis submersus.*

1877   Begins correspondence with Gottfried Keller.

1878   *Carsten Curator; Renate.*

1879   *Eekenhof.*

1880   Retires from the bench and moves to the village of Hademarschen.

1882   *Hans und Heinz Kirch;* the young Germanist Erich Schmidt visits him.

1883   *Schweigen.*

1884   Trip to Berlin and last meeting with Fontane; *Zur Chronik von Grieshuus.*

1885   *John Riew; Ein Fest auf Haderslevhuus.*

1886   Trip to Weimar; death of his firstborn son Hans; *Ein Doppelgänger.*

1887   September 14: Public celebration of his seventieth birthday in Husum; *Ein Bekenntnis.*

1888   *Der Schimmelreiter;* July 4: Storm dies in Hademarschen and is interred in the family crypt in Husum.

CHAPTER 1

The Life of the Poet

I *Husum*

THEODOR WOLDSEN STORM was born on September 14, 1817, in Husum, a town in the duchy of Schleswig. Since the duchies of Schleswig-Holstein had been a part of Denmark since 1773, and since Schleswig remained Danish until 1864, Storm was by birth a Danish citizen (or a "Schuckelmeyer," as the Danes were called by their political enemies).[1] On the distaff side, the Woldsen family, Storm belonged to one of Husum's old families of well-to-do traders with their own fleet of ships. The stately house of his maternal grandparents—an eighteenth-century structure of rustic Rococo architecture—with its many mementos of a patrician past, formed a lasting impression on the boy. The portraits of his ancestors, the family vault nearby, and the stories and anecdotes about his family were vivid reminders of his own identity and shaped his consciousness of an honored tradition. From the house and the Rococo artefacts it contained, Storm himself traced his preference for the idyllic aspect of that period. The vignettes *Im Sonnenschein* (In the Sunshine) (1854), *Im Saal* (In the Hall) (1848), *Zwei Kuchenesser der alten Zeit* (Two Cake Eaters of Old) (1871), and *Der Amtschirurgus* (The Public Health Surgeon) (1871) take place in the middle of the eighteenth century and were inspired by memories of his youth spent in the Woldsen house on the Hohle Gasse in Husum.[2]

It is perhaps no accident that Storm wrote these stories many years later, when—once again—memory had imbued the recollection of all he had heard and seen with a gentle glow and some nostalgia. Happiness for Storm always existed in some distant past, rarely in the present, and there are only a few poems or novellas which do not entail a reminiscence and the accompanying feeling of an irretrievable loss. Perhaps, typically, Storm's preference for the Rococo was a highly selective one which permitted

13

an effective escape from the unpleasant political and social realities of his own time. Storm ignored the philosophers and writers of the Enlightenment, and of the French and American revolutions, preferring the more idyllic aspects of the period exemplified by the etchings of bucolic subjects by Daniel Chodowiecki, Salomon Gessner's *Idyls,* the Anacreontic poets, and the poets of the *Göttinger Hain.*

Recalling his background and family ties, Storm wrote from his voluntary exile in Potsdam in 1853:

The strong attachment to my native land, the impossibility, felt more strongly every day, to acclimatize elsewhere (especially here) may be connected with the fact that my ancestors on both sides have lived in the home town or in the hereditary country homes for centuries; and I grew up fully conscious of that fact, and as if it could not be otherwise. In Husum I lived, so to speak, in an atmosphere of venerable family traditions; almost every family of craftsmen in town had, in one generation or another, a servant or maid working for our family; the names of my ancestors were closely linked with the good old days, when my greatgrandfather, the old merchant Friedrich Woldsen, had an ox slaughtered every year for the poor. Through both her parents, my mother belongs to the old patrician families of Husum which no longer survive, but from which had descended, for many centuries, the successful businessmen, lawyers, and mayors of our good city. Since the male branch of the Woldsen family had expired in the main line, I was christened "Woldsen Storm" in order to preserve the name.[3]

On his father's side, Theodor Storm was descended from a long line of millers and farmers resident in Westermühlen near Husum. His father had studied law and settled in Husum in 1815 as a lawyer. He was soon to become a very popular and highly respected jurist in the area. Just as the Woldsen home and its tradition had had a deep influence on Storm's sense of identity, so did Westermühlen, the home of his paternal grandparents: "This word evokes in me an entire forest and milling idyl; the small village nestled behind bushes and trees was the birthplace and home of my father. . . ."[4] "Westermühlen" (one of his earliest poems) and "Abseits" reflect some of the natural beauty of this peaceful idyl of his youth.

In past centuries, the town of Husum had been a fairly important port city and trade center on the North Sea. At the time of Storm's birth, however, it was a small provincial backwater, offering no great opportunities to the ambitious and certainly none to the culturally and intellectually inclined. Thus, in 1835, Storm's parents decided to send their son to the *Katharineum* in Lübeck to complete his secondary education. The *Gelehrtenschule* in Husum, which he had attended until then, offered very limited and mediocre instruction, especially in modern German literature, as Storm once ruefully remarked. In Lübeck he made the acquaintance of the young Emanuel Geibel whom he was to call, in later years, his poetic antithesis. The most consequential encounter during his two years at the *Katharineum* was that with Ferdinand Röse, who introduced Theodor to Goethe's *Faust*, to the contemporary German poets, and, above all, to Heinrich Heine's *Buch der Lieder* and Eichendorff's lyrics. Eduard Mörike's poetry, which Storm discovered for himself, together with Heine's and Eichendorff's, furnished the models for his first attempts at writing poetry. Storm and Röse became close friends. As a memorial to their friendship, Storm dedicated a poem to Röse in which the latter appears under the humorous nickname of Magister Anton Wanst.

While staying with relatives in Altona near Hamburg, Storm made the acquaintance of Bertha von Buchan, a ten-year-old child who was living with her foster mother. He took an instant liking to the girl. Subsequently, he corresponded with her, sending her songs, riddles, and fairy tales. It was at first, the child which attracted him, and he delighted in offering his poetic products to the innocent imagination of a child. Gradually, however, during his second stay in Kiel, Storm fell deeply in love with Bertha, and in 1842 he asked formally for her hand in marriage. Bertha, who was then sixteen, refused. Storm wrote, "Born of my own heart, never possessed, yet lost." [5] The poems reflecting his feelings for Bertha mark the point at which Storm found his individual style as a writer of love poetry. The artistic sublimation of this unhappy experience helped him to overcome it. Bertha also provided the impetus for the novella *Immensee*, a lyrical story of unrequited love. The best of the Bertha von Buchan poems Storm included in the first volume of his poetry, *Liederbuch dreier Freunde*, 1843: "You are so young—they call you a child— / If you love me, you hardly know yourself. / You will forget me and these hours, / And when you turn around and I am gone, / It will seem to you overnight as in a dream / . . . ." [6] Two years after Bertha and Storm had parted company, Storm became engaged to Constanze Esmarch, whom he married in 1846.

Another important influence on his later years as a writer was the unmarried daughter of a baker in Husum, Magdalena Jürgens, called Lena Wies, who was twenty years his senior. From her he not only heard many folk tales and stories of his native Schleswig-Holstein, but she was also instrumental in sparking his poetic imagination. She strengthened his skeptical attitude toward religion, and Storm expressed himself on that subject in a letter to the Hebbel biographer, Emil Kuh.[7] In the reminiscent tale *Lena Wies* (1870), there is a line spoken by the dying woman which Storm was very fond of quoting: "Well, Reverend, you won't get *me!*" [8]

Since his father wanted him to become a lawyer and since Storm had by no means determined that his artistic interests were in any sense exclusive, he enrolled in 1837, after his graduation from the *Katharineum,* in the Law School at the University of Kiel. The atmosphere at the university was not to his liking, however. He scorned the provincialism of this small-town school and the mindless activities of the drinking and dueling fraternities. In several of his early novellas, Storm gave expression to his disdain for these exclusive yet vacuous organizations.

Thus, after a year, Storm decided to move to Berlin in order to continue his studies there. The fact that Ferdinand Röse was a student at the Friedrich-Wilhelm Universität was decisive. Visits to the theater, art galleries, and a circle of art-minded friends who had gathered around Röse added immensely to Storm's sense of well-being. Although the list of famous names on the faculty of the university was considerable, Storm attended only the lectures of Karl von Savigny, the founder of the school of historical jurisprudence. After Röse's departure from Berlin, he returned to Kiel in 1839.

Back in Kiel, Storm became a member of the circle around Theodor Mommsen, who was destined to become one of Germany's foremost classical historians. Their chief interest concerned literature. The "Book of Songs of three Friends" (1843) was one of the many tangible results of that association. The gathering of folk and fairy tales, legends, and critical reviews for newspapers filled Storm's time away from his studies.

In October, 1842, Storm passed his examination and returned to his home town to work in his father's law office. In December,

1842, he applied to Christian VIII, king of Denmark, for a license to practice law in the duchies of Schleswig-Holstein, stating that he could read, speak, and translate Danish without difficulty. In 1843 he opened his own office as an attorney-at-law in Husum. Until his retirement in 1879, he pursued a successful legal career as a lawyer, judge, chief of police, and administrative official. Aside from the necessity of having to earn a living, which the sale of his writings could never provide, Storm believed in the separation of artistic endeavors from the rigors and duties of a responsible position and function in society. He wrote to the young writer, Heinrich Seidel, who had given up his post as an engineer in order to devote himself exclusively to writing: "I know from my own experience how much poetic production gains and is supported by work which is different and completely separate from it. Indeed, it is more profitable for poetic production if it receives only the hour favorable to it rather than the joy of everyday labors in the workshop." [9] There was never any real conflict between the demands of Storm's bourgeois existence and his artistic calling. Whatever his criticisms of the world he lived in and even his prophetic insights into the slow decline of a secure patriarchal and middle-class society, he could and would not deny his middle-class origins and obligations. His art was an integral part of that world, representing it in order to "move deeply" and to preserve and assign a total meaning to life despite all evidence to the contrary.

Storm's life in Husum was devoted to his profession and to the city choir which he had founded. After a two-year period of engagement, Storm and Constanze Esmarch, the daughter of the mayor of Segeberg, were married. The extensive correspondence with his fiancée shows Storm's feelings for Constanze to have been less than passionate; rather they grew steadily as their relationship became closer and more intimate. The correspondence, above all, proves the young poet and advocate to be a severe taskmaster and idealist where his bride-to-be was concerned. He perpetually tried to educate and improve her mind much to his subsequent regret, when he confessed to her how wrong he had been in torturing and nagging her, who had always loved him, never showing any impatience or anger. Their marriage in 1846 was soon to be put to a severe test. Dorothea Jensen, a friend of one of his sisters in Husum, kindled his passion. She seems to have possessed all those qualities which Storm did not find in Constanze. Storm's most passionate love lyric was prompted by and dedicated to Dorothea. "Mysterium," published only long after the poet's death, reveals the nature of their relationship:

> Kein Ungestüm und kein Verzagen;
> Sie löste Gürtel und Gewand
> Und gab sich feierlich und schweigend
> Und hülflos in der Liebe Hand.[10]

(No impetuousness and no despair; she loosened girth and gown and surrendered solemnly and silently and helplessly to love.)

Dorothea left Husum in 1848. After Constanze's death in 1865, she became Theodor Storm's second wife in 1866.

At this point it may be necessary to dispel the notion that Theodor Storm's affair with Dorothea Jensen was sufficiently disreputable to make him an unconventional member of his social class in keeping with the behavior expected of a famous artist. The issue has often been distorted in the accounts of literary historians and Storm scholarship for at least two reasons. One was that Gertrud Storm, his youngest daughter, became the curator of her father's literary estate. In an effort to preserve as favorable as possible an image of the poet, she withheld a good deal of evidence concerning this particular juncture in his life.[11] Thus, for example, the lines from "Mysterium" quoted above represent only one stanza besides two others published before 1956, when the remaining five came to light. Similarly, the letter addressed to his friend Hartmuth Brinkmann, in which he confessed his reasons for his later marriage to Dorothea, was omitted from Gertrud Storm's edition:[12] "In my young marriage, one ingredient was missing: passion. Mine and Constanze's hands had remained linked more in the quiet assurance of a liking for each other . . . but about that child was that intoxicating atmosphere which I could not resist."[13] The love lyric which had sprung from this experience moves between expressions of passion and joy and renunciation and remorse symbolized, respectively, by red and white roses. On the other hand, in an effort to rescue and defend Storm's image as that of a complex and profound artistic person, Thomas Mann, too, overemphasized and, hence, distorted the significance of the love affair. He wrote in 1930 that Storm had lived behind a façade of respectability and that his infidelity proves once more the precarious role of the artist in bourgeois society. He sought to refute the argument that Storm was no more than a somewhat pedestrian writer of harmless stories with regional setting and local color whose life had been equally bland.[14] These ideas had been most prominently advocated by Theodor Fontane (although he modified them later) and Emil Ermatinger. Since the appearance of Mann's essay, hardly an opportunity has been lost by well-meaning Storm critics to point to Thomas Mann's spirited defense of their poet. We know, however, that Storm suffered greatly from his infidelity and paid the price with severe pangs of self-recrimination and remorse. He saw his problem as one arising from a conflict between his passionate nature and his middle-class conscience. He and Dorothea decided to resolve it in favor of accepted social behavior. The aftermath of this experience in his life was not only visible in his poetry of that time but also in some of the novellas concerning the problem of marriage, most prominently so in *Veronika* (1861) and *Viola tricolor* (Wild Pansy) (1873). *Veronika* concerns the infidelity of a wife and the absolution of her guilt by her husband after her confession. She is freed from her guilt by her complete candor toward him and by an implicit trust and faith in him. The title of the other story alludes to the German word for pansy, which also means stepmother. The second wife of a man, as well as his young daughter, finds it almost impossible to compete with the memory of his first wife. The little girl and her father treat her as a stepmother, and it takes understanding and the practical will to overcome the memory of the past and to accept what is necessary and right: to live as a true family and to establish a loving bond between stepmother and stepchild. The symbol for this story is the flower garden which the husband had kept under lock ever since the death of his first wife, who used to tend it. After the happy resolution, the rusty lock of the gate is broken and the family enters the "garden of the past," the symbol of love and neglect, to cultivate it once more and to affirm their faith in a happy future. The problems that Storm and Dorothea were facing in the first two years of their marriage found their artistic representation in this story.

Marriage was of central importance to Storm. He clearly saw the problem as one involving a conflict between an individual's inclinations and society's right to demand a strict legal definition

of the union of man and woman. His own experience of this conflict could only reinforce his resolve to defend the institution of
marriage as a moral obligation implicit in matrimony which is
"the sanctity of form having become the accepted custom." [15]
Storm saw the family as the nucleus and basis of any state, which
can only be dissolved by the common will, that is, by the law. This
austere, middle-class concept—or more precisely, this *Biedermeier* concept—of matrimony, also had its roots in his strong ties
to his own wife and children. To him, familial love was a bastion
against a grim world. It offered the only possibility of self-
expression and self-perpetuation through one's children. It is no
exaggeration to say that in the absence of a belief in any other
meaningful reality transcending the individual, such as the nation-
state or religion, the individual and his family were the only cer-
tainties remaining.

How deeply Storm cared for his family—as for his homeland—
is also evident from the infinite patience he showed with regard to
his children. The suffering caused him by his oldest son, Hans,
and his youngest son, Karl, is vividly expressed in his letters to
Paul Heyse and in two novellas. Just as *Viola tricolor, Carsten
Curator* (Curator Carsten) (1877) and *Ein stiller Musikant* (A
Quiet Musician) (1875) are confessional in character and deal
with problems arising in the lives of two of his sons. Hans, an alcoholic, was of weak and unstable character and died as a young
man. The problem of heredity and alcoholism preoccupied Storm
as much as anyone in his day. Curator Carsten's son suffers a similar fate. Karl, a mediocre musician, lacked the will power and the
talent to be more than an obscure small-town piano teacher. The
novella describes the life of such an obscure musician. Storm not
only suffered from thoughts of any possible omission on his
part in the upbringing of his children; he also despaired over the
seeming cruelty of life which presented itself to him and many of
his contemporaries (especially the later Naturalists) as a relentless and merciless mechanism creating biological facts over which
no man had any control. Thus, as he was fond of saying, a kind
of "culpa patris" was at work, as well as an original sin whose
manifestation was a form of visitation of genetic evils, from an
obscure beginning in the distant past, on innocent and hapless
descendants.

II *Potsdam*

In the course of the political struggles of 1848, Schleswig-Holstein attempted to secede from Denmark, and a provisional government for the duchies was established in Rendsburg. In the ensuing military operations, Prussian and other troops of the German Federation ousted the Danes from these northernmost German territories. Storm's political poems, as well as his contributions to Theodor Mommsen's *Schleswig-Holsteinische Zeitung*,[16] express his patriotism. His attitude was essentially democratic, anti-Danish, antiaristocratic, and anticlerical. However, he considered himself basically apolitical, and it is true that he did not have more than a rudimentary idea about a future organization of the body politic. After Prussia and Denmark had concluded an armistice in 1849 and a peace treaty in the following year, the troops of the duchies proved too weak to resist the overwhelming strength of the Danes. In 1851 Schleswig was reoccupied by Denmark and Holstein by Austria. The signatories of the London Protocol of 1852 guaranteed the unified succession of the Danish monarchy to the duchies in the interests of Europe. As an outspoken and implacable foe of the Danes, Storm had his license to practice law revoked by the Danish authorities in Schleswig-Holstein. In 1853, Storm wrote "Abschied" (Farewell) which expresses the painful feelings that accompanied his decision to leave his beloved homeland. "We are parting now until the burdens of these times / Have been vindicated by another day, a better day / For now there is only room on our soil / For the foreigners and for what serves their needs." And to his newborn son, he addressed the lines: "And you, my child, my youngest . . . hear me! For all else is but a lie— / No man thrives without a fatherland!" [17]

Desperate and unfamiliar with Prussian law, Storm nevertheless accepted an unpaid position as an assistant judge at the district court in Potsdam. His own parents and his wife's parents had to support him even when, after eight months, the court finally paid him an extremely meager per diem allowance which was not even sufficient to pay the rent. In the beginning, he had no time for his art. There was also his increasing annoyance with Prussian ways. He could not abide the frugality and brutality of the governmental apparatus. His apartment, his family, and his friends were his refuge in those days. He made the personal acquaintance of Joseph von Eichendorff, which was a big event for him who had admired the poet for so long and whose poetry had been so strongly influenced by his. The other personal encounter of importance at the time was that with Eduard Mörike, the revered poet and mentor, to whom Storm paid a visit on a trip to Heidelberg and Stuttgart.

During his stay in Potsdam, Storm belonged to two literary societies called "Tunnel über der Spree" (Tunnel above the river Spree) and the "Rütli." Theodor Fontane, Paul Heyse, Franz Kugler, Friedrich Eggers, and the famous painter Adolf Menzel also belonged to the latter group. Fontane, in slightly ironic tones, reports about these gatherings in his autobiography *Von Zwanzig bis Dreissig*. The purpose of these gatherings was the critical discussion of literature as well as recitations from the production of the individual members. Theodor Fontane describes one typical Storm recitation, giving us, in his somewhat matter-of-fact and ironic manner, his impression of this very "poetic poet" who seemed so ill at ease among all these self-assured Prussians:

When the moment to begin the recitation had come, he would be agitated and embarrassed—not from shyness but because his eye, scanning the room, did not yet find everything as he wanted it. There was the maid still rattling the plates, there were two men still sitting in a corner more preoccupied with themselves than with Storm, there was the hand of the clock pointing at five minutes of eleven, so that he could calculate exactly that when the climax was reached the moment would also have come for the clock to strike eleven times. But then the whole effect would be ruined. The worst for him, however, was the thought of the sudden appearance of someone during the recitation to report the arrival of the carriage or the like. That was deadly for him. But the hostesses knew and were not surprised when he arose to bolt all the doors. Then he lowered the lamp a bit to further enhance the atmosphere, and now he was reading. Well, and how! No one has ever read like that. He knew the things by heart and had set them to music, so to speak. . . .[18]

Only two of his novellas were written during the Potsdam years. One of them, *Angelika* (1854), represents the poetic sublimation of the Dorothea experience. Angelika, like Dorothea, speaks of an innate or predestined love for one man, and, like Dorothea, she refuses all of her suitors, remaining faithful to the only man she has ever loved.

In the summer of 1856, Storm finally succeeded in obtaining a position that promised not only adequate pay but also the peaceful life in a small town which Storm always considered essential for a feeling of well-being. He and his family moved to Heiligenstadt, a Catholic town in the province of Thuringia and seat of the district court where Storm was to be the judge.

III *Heiligenstadt*

It did not take very long for Storm to feel at home in the small Prussian provincial backwater. During the almost eight years of exile in Heiligenstadt, Storm's family grew to six children whose number eventually increased to eight after his second marriage. With a large family to support, his salary soon became inadequate, and he had to have his parents' subsidies as well as the flat fees from his books to keep his finances in any sort of order.

Storm's active interest in music soon established him as an expert in the small community. He founded a choir, and he and Constanze also functioned as soloists. His own compositions as well as those of the great composers of art songs were part of the repertoire.

Ludwig Pietsch, graphic artist and art critic for the *Vossische Zeitung* in Berlin, became a close friend of Storm's and provided the illustrations for many of his novellas. His descriptions of the cultural life in Heiligenstadt tell us that the Storm family set the tone by their recitations of literature and music. The administrative head of the district, Alexander von Wussow, a man of great knowledge and intelligence, became one of Storm's confidants and partners in his discussions about art and politics. As a member of the Prussian aristocracy, von Wussow was remarkably unpretentious and tolerant. Given Storm's very vocal opposition to the nobility, the relationship would not have endured had von Wussow's attitudes been less humane.

Storm's prose production in "exile" demonstrates his progress from the early, purely "atmospheric" or lyrical novellas such as *Immensee* to a more resolute narrative perspective. Although his stories deal almost exclusively with reminiscences from his homeland, he attained a more detached perspective of his material and even engaged in social criticism, as in the story *Im Schloss* (1861). Hinrich Arnold, the main character of the novella, is proud of his humble origins and does not feel inferior to the aristocrats of his social environment. The novella provoked considerable criticism among Storm's aristocratic readers, and he expressed the fear that he might have lost his following among the nobility. Storm wrote a total of nine novellas during his years in Heiligenstadt and also edited the *Anthology of German Love Lyric since Christian Günther*. His poetic production was limited to epigrams and some political poetry, written before his return to Husum in 1863 and 1864, when the military and political struggle in Schleswig-Holstein had once more—and for the last time—reached the point of open conflict. Apart from a handful of poems and private statements on the subject, Storm avoided any active participation in the liberation of Schleswig-Holstein as well as in the struggle against the vestiges of aristocratic rule in Germany, and that in spite of his desire to become a second "Tyrtaios of Sparta" fighting with his poetry for democracy. Instead, he began to withdraw and turned to the writing of fairy tales, which he completed after his return to Husum. Three of his five fairy tales were written during the years 1863–64.

Since the Danes sought to annex Schleswig outright by proclaiming their constitution as valid there, and since the London agreements stipulated that the two duchies must remain unified, the situation in the North became critical. The accession to the throne of Christian IX on November 15, 1863, further aggravated the affair. Thus the Federation of German States sent troops to the duchies in support of the provisional government which had, in the meantime, been formed by the rebellious Schleswig-Holsteiners. The struggle was closely followed by all liberal-minded Germans, since it was hoped that it would bring about German unity and produce a kind of republic of independent, democratically ruled states. Storm's hopes were leaning strongly in that direction. Prince Friedrich of Augustenburg, the ruling prince of the duchies, did not recognize the London treaty either and declared himself the sovereign over these territories. Prussia and Austria now intervened to oust the prince and to prevent any one German state from gaining preeminence. Since the Danes threatened to upset the balance of power in these northern states, Prussia and Austria declared war on Denmark. The federal troops from Hanover and Saxony withdrew to allow the bigger powers to decide the outcome. Early in 1864 the Prusso-Austrian army defeated the Danes, and the duchies became a Prussian province.

The people of Schleswig-Holstein, who fervently wished to be free and independent, were soon to be disappointed in their hopes, because of the authoritarian sway the Prussians held over their new province. In the heady days of revolt and after the victory over the Danes, the pro-Danish chief of police and judge of the Husum district had been ousted and the question "who shall be 'Landvogt'?" was now resolved by the town meeting in favor of Theodor Storm. The office of Landvogt was an old and highly respected one going back to the days of independence and near-democratic government in the duchies. It was an elective office combining the functions of civil and criminal court judge as well as chief law enforcement officer. Storm's father, a highly respected and trusted lawyer who had practiced law in Husum for fifty years, was the main reason for his son's election by the people, who trusted the reputation of the name and who voted for him in his absence. Storm was to be the last Landvogt of Husum. The Prussian ministry of justice abolished the office three years later in 1867.

When the news of his appointment reached Storm in February 1864, he is said to have exclaimed to his family, "whom of you shall I have to sacrifice for this?" [19] as if he had learned not to trust his good fortune. His pessimistic question was to be answered in a terrible way one year later, when Constanze died of puerperal fever after the birth of their seventh child.

IV *Husum and Hademarschen*

Constanze's death in May, 1865, was Storm's most shattering experience. He believed that he was at the end of his ability to write: "I am afraid that the power of poetic productivity has been laid to rest forever along with her; for never, when I was far from her, did I write a single line, except for a few verses prompted by my longing for her. When her hand held me fast on homeland soil, then I could rise without a care to the lofty regions of the imagination. . . ." [20] This gloomy mood of despair was gradually overcome. One year later, Dorothea Jensen became his wife. The first years of his second marriage were difficult, because Storm had, in the meantime, made a cult of Constanze's memory. He even forbade his children to call their stepmother anything except "Aunt Do." Only after the birth of his eighth (her first) child in 1868, was Dorothea accepted by the entire family.

In the summer of 1865, in order to take his mind off his sorrow, he decided to travel, leaving his children in the care of Miss Pyle, an English governess. Storm traveled to Baden-Baden to follow the invitation of Ivan Turgenev, with whom he had been corresponding and who valued Storm's novellas highly. The famous French singer Pauline Viardot-Garcia, who had accompanied Turgenev, introduced Storm to a world whose elegance and sophistication were completely alien to his thinking and experience. Soirées and recitals, attended by the Queen of Prussia and her court, seemed far removed from the simplicity of life in Husum. This completely different environment and Turgenev's generous friendship, as well as the intelligent conversations, concerts, and social occasions made the poet forget his cares, and he returned to Husum in September, visibly refreshed.

After the abolition of Storm's office, he had the choice between an administrative or a judicial post. He chose to be a judge once more because of the greater measure of independence it afforded. In spite of the fact that Storm intensely disliked the Prussians, he gradually came to terms with his professional duties and managed to organize his working day in such a way that he could write and socialize regularly. It did not take long, therefore, before he was again as active as he had been in Heiligenstadt. His circle of friends was naturally larger. Just as in Heiligenstadt, he found in the administrative head of the region, Count Reventlow, a friend and art-minded person. Storm's correspondence with Gottfried Keller and Emil Kuh, the Hebbel biographer, his friendship with the fellow Schleswiger and Low German dialect poet, Klaus Groth, as well as with the literary star of the time, Paul Heyse, the Germanist Erich Schmidt, and other writers and scholars prove his serious and intense interests in many areas of culture and the respect he had earned for himself as an artist.

After a period of barrenness and rest, Storm began to write again in 1870. The events that took place in Germany at that time he only acknowledged in his correspondence. Storm's contempt for Bismarck and his ruthless policies only reinforced his resolve to seek a world of esthetic beauty and avoid any contact with that of politics. The 1870's mark the gradual progression from the novellas of quiet renunciation to those dealing with tragic themes. His second anthology of German poetry, *Hausbuch aus deutschen*

Dichtern seit Claudius, appeared in 1870, although its reception by the public and the critics was disappointing. The period of his so-called chronicle novellas began after 1875. It produced stories based on fictitious documents which provide the frame and then, by flashback, the main body of the narrative. Thus the high point of his writings was reached with his first masterpiece, the "chronicle novella" *Aquis Submersus* (1876).[21]

As early as 1868, Georg Westermann had published Storm's collected works in an edition of six volumes. One of his chief complaints about the publication of his works had been the fairly small financial return on his efforts. Now, with increasing fame and mastery of his craft, Storm commanded prices that only the best writers of the time could expect. Thus he was able to provide an expensive education for all his growing children, a matter of great importance to him.

Storm was a conscientious worker, and he gradually rose in the judicial hierarchy of this newest and last Prussian province. The only consistent sorrow and burden in that happy and successful decade of his life was the plight of his oldest son Hans. He was a hopeless alcoholic who—after years of struggling—finally managed to pass his examinations in medicine with the active help of his father. He saw in him the victim of a tragic chain of genetic events stemming from some distant forebear. He also saw in him a child "gone astray" whom he had to protect, as indeed he would have done for any of his children. "You are without peace, my poor son, / And I am without peace because of you. . . ." are the opening lines of a poem about Hans.[22] After several years of service as a ship's doctor, Hans died of alcoholism at the age of thirty-eight.

In 1879, Storm's mother died, and he was now the heir to the old family residence on the Hohle Gasse. Instead of moving his family there, however, he decided to sell the house and make a new beginning. He requested early retirement from his judgeship and decided to build a house in the country where he could devote all of his time to writing and to his family and circle of friends.

In 1880, the Ministry of Justice in Berlin retired Theodor Storm with the title of "Amtsgerichtsrat" (councilor) and he was awarded a medal for his service to his country. Storm moved into his last residence in April, 1881. The village of Hademarschen in Holstein, thus, was to be his place of retirement. These last years of his life mark the apex of his literary career.

From Hademarschen, Storm traveled once more to Berlin, where he met with Theodor Fontane for the last time. Two years later, in 1886, he also traveled to Weimar. In both cities he was received and celebrated as one of Germany's outstanding writers. Recognition had come slowly for him, but for this reason "all the more durably," as Storm put it. His seventieth birthday, therefore, was a truly popular occasion. The entire village turned out to celebrate the poet in their midst; the city of Husum had already made him an "Honorary Citizen" (a considerable honor which included such privileges as tax-exempt status); and valuable gifts and tokens of love and esteem reached him from all parts of the country. "How wonderful, that I did not pass away last year, so I could at last hear from others what I had known about myself for forty years . . . ," he wrote in the last year of his life.[23] Storm's reference here was to his literary fame and to his final illness, which had been diagnosed as abdominal cancer. The effect of this finding on him proved very depressing, indeed. Thus it was decided by the members of his immediate family to induce his brother Aemil, who was a physician, to reexamine the patient. The fictitious result of this examination, which was conducted with the knowledge of the attending physician, was to declare the previous finding erroneous and to assign a harmless name to his ailment. The effect on Storm was almost immediate. He could rally sufficient strength to finish his last and most significant work, *Der Schimmelreiter* (The White Horse Rider), in the spring of 1888. A few months later, on July 4, 1888, his life came to an end. He was buried in the family crypt in Husum with people from far and near attending the funeral. Neither a priest nor a friend spoke at his grave. It was his last wish to be buried in silence, as an ultimate acknowledgment of the irrevocable power of death to which there was no answer.

CHAPTER 2

Storm's Lyric Poetry

I The Editions

ALTHOUGH Theodor Storm's poetry commands an almost equal place with his prose writings, the total number of poems is only somewhere near three hundred, filling a slender volume. Storm himself regarded his lyric poetry as more important than his prose, as he wrote to his publisher, Georg Westermann, in 1868, "Essentially, I am a lyric poet, and my human and poetic personality, my character, passion, and humor are only wholly and completely reflected in my poetry. In my prose works the limits are defined much more narrowly." [1]

During his lifetime, his poems were published in only seven editions. At the same time, the vastly inferior poetry of Emanuel Geibel, for instance, appeared in one hundred and twenty editions.[2] Storm was extremely critical of his own production, and he carefully supervised the publication of his poems, screening out what he regarded as inferior or, on occasion, as untimely. The earliest beginnings of his poetic endeavors date from his childhood in 1829. Little that he wrote prior to 1843 was deemed worthy by him of inclusion in the first publication of his poetry, which was a joint edition of the poems by Theodor Storm and his friends, the brothers Theodor and Tycho Mommsen, a small volume entitled *Liederbuch dreier Freunde.*

Storm's personal copy of the *Liederbuch* of 1843 [3] contains five pages in the back of the book with additional stanzas for two of his poems ("Fiedellieder" and "Repos d'amour") in his own handwriting; similarly, the table of contents shows his marks indicating the poems he had selected for inclusion in the first edition of his poetry in 1852. These emendations by his own hand attest to a continuous critical concern with his lyric poetry as well as to the fact that some of the poems of the 1843 edition were not included in the first separate edition of 1852 (*Gedichte*). Although the last edition of his poems during his lifetime appeared in 1885, three years before his death, his golden period as a poet occurred in the early years of his literary career. He was an accomplished poet long before he had reached a similar stage in his prose writings. For the purpose of orientation, Franz Stuckert's division of Storm's lyric poetry into three distinct phases may be useful.[4] These divisions provide for the periods from 1843 to 1854, 1854 to 1867, and 1870 to 1885. In order for this to have any meaning at all, it should be pointed out that the years between 1852 and 1854 were by far the most productive in both quantity and quality.

The first collection of 1852 already constitutes a program that Storm was merely to elaborate on in greater detail in his correspondence over the years and that he was to realize by way of his two anthologies of German poetry. The poems that have survived expurgation from the joint 1843 edition are truly his own in tone and mood and no longer chiefly indebted to the influence of Goethe, Heine, Mörike, and Eichendorff. The collection opens with a convivial poem called "Oktoberlied" (1848) which Storm regarded as an "immortal poem." It is clear from its position in the collection that he meant it to be an affirmation of life (considering the date, one might think of the revolution as a backdrop: "Und geht es draussen noch so toll. / Unchristlich oder christlich / Ist doch die Welt . . . / So gänzlich unverwüstlich" [No matter how bad things are out there, Christian or unchristian, the world is indestructible]). As a convivial song, it belongs to the artistically minor category of a medieval "Ständelied" and is, in spite of Storm's high esteem for it, one of the lesser examples of his poetry and also rather untypical of his thematic bent.[5] In another respect, however, it is unmistakably Stormian in the note of fear it contains, which is drowned out by noisy conviviality ending in a *carpe diem* mood typical of much of Storm's poetry, as well as of his philosophy of life. The collection closes with the "epilogue," so designated by the poet, in the form of the poem "In hoc signo vinces." Chiefly by way of the lyrical address or invocation, the poem describes the conscious and courageous acceptance of death and the overcoming of the fear of death. The middle portion of the anthology contains three of Storm's fairy-tale poems. This part is prefaced by the programmatic verses "Märchen" (Fairy Tales), an apology for the genre, which is reminiscent, in style and theme, of the late Romantic poet Joseph von Eichendorff. The final part comprises Storm's poems written between 1840 and 1843.

The entire volume was intended to be read consecutively, from cover to cover. The first part (his lyric from 1843 to 1852) contains the entire range of Storm's poetic themes, that is, mostly love, nature, transiency, and death. In its entirety, then, the anthology conveys the impression of an affirmation of life over death in spite of the many threats to which it is exposed.

II *Between Reality and Illusion: Storm's Lyrical Canon and the Structure and Form of his Lyric Poetry*

Two statements from Storm's many comments on his lyrical art may stand for all the others. In an unpublished draft of a letter to Miss Helene Clark, the first English translator of *Immensee*, Storm wrote "That which, in part, lends value to my poetry and determines its effect is, I believe, its strict simplicity of expression and its objectivity, i.e., concreteness of representation. I have always tried to express the subject matter itself rather than, simultaneously, its effect on the mind of the reader; the latter, in fact, must come about by itself." [6] And in a letter to his friend Hartmuth Brinkmann, he once remarked: "The art of lyrical poetry consists in expressing as general a meaning as possible through as individual a form as possible." [7] Both statements paradigmatically point to the peculiar problem that follows from them for his poetry as well his esthetic theories. The "objectivity" programmatically stated in the two excerpts above shows the dilemma of the "realist," forced to create a hypostatized truth where there is only the individual phenomenon and the isolated truth. Thus Storm is compelled to make a virtue out of necessity and declare, by way of his lyrical canon, that any poem worth the name must be based on an experience and an occasion, accompanied by a strong emotion. For the sake of an illusory "objective" reality that binds the subjective experience to some "higher" form outside it, Storm is content with a limited formal range for his poetry; the only yardstick that is to be applied to it is the test of the "immediacy" of its emotional content.

Even in his political poems, relating to specific historical events of the day, Storm sought to render their meaning as "general" as he could, and he would, on occasion, rewrite them to expurgate what might seem too specific to be profoundly "true" and capable of being experienced beyond the moment to which its occasion may have given rise. In his poetry as well as in his prose, the normative categories are chiefly transiency and a firm belief in an ethical or esthetic value system. The individual phenomenon is considered as the part that signifies the whole, bound to the illusion of an "objective" reality outside the "subjective" by either a psychological or an empirical nexus. The personal experience of the lyrical self (or that of the narrator in the novella) must be explicable and justified by some kind of connection between itself and the hypostatized totality which exists only in the mind of the poet.

Storm's esthetic theories reflect the vacillation, present in his poetry, between an ethical world view, whose frame of reference is Husum and the people of northern Frisia, and a purely esthetic as well as, occasionally, an irrational point of view. The latter vantage point is most prominent in his poems dealing with the supernatural or even the occult.[8]

The vulgar materialism of his age could never be a substitute for Storm's acute sense of loss of a meaningful totality. On the contrary, it served to reinforce his despair over a hopelessly fragmented reality, apparently signifying nothing but itself. The chief expression of his "torment" (as it has been called in another context)[9] is that of sustaining a miraculous unity of spirit and nature, of God and the world—characterizing the genre of the folk song and lyrical song—and, simultaneously, retaining the natural objectivity of the genre of the proverb or saying. In Storm's epigrammatic lyrics (chiefly his political and "philosophic" poems) the view of the world is "pantheistic" or "esthetic," centering about the fact that the isolated individual is at its core, and the cosmic view is no more than an afterthought, a painful and tormenting one, to be sure.

In the prerevolutionary period or "Vormärz" of 1847, the poet wrote "Abseits" (Refuge), a poem which describes a peaceful idyl, removed from the turmoil of the present. He gives us an image of nature at the noon hour of a warm summer day. The landscape is Storm's native heath. The poet gazes at a ramshackle house and its owner, a beekeeper, sitting by the open door, dreaming of his harvests of honey. The last two verses abruptly

take the reader and listener away from the idyllic scene with a
reflection upon the climate of the times.

Abseits

Es ist so still; die Heide liegt
Im warmen Mittagssonnenstrahle,
Ein rosenroter Schimmer fliegt
Um ihre alten Gräbermale;
Die Kräuter blühn; der Heideduft
Steigt in die blaue Sommerluft.

Laufkäfer hasten durchs Gesträuch
In ihren goldnen Panzerröckchen,
Die Bienen hängen Zweig um Zweig
Sich an der Edelheide Glöckchen,
Die Vögel schwirren aus dem Kraut—
Die Luft ist voller Lerchenlaut.

Ein halbverfallen niedrig Haus
Steht einsam hier und sonnbeschienen;
Der Kätner lehnt zur Tür hinaus,
Behaglich blinzelnd nach den Bienen;
Sein Junge auf dem Stein davor
Schnitzt Pfeifen sich aus Kälberrohr.

Kaum zittert durch die Mittagsruh
Ein Schlag der Dorfuhr, der entfernten;
Dem Alten fällt die Wimper zu,
Er träumt von seinen Honigernten.
—Kein Klang der aufgeregten Zeit
Drang noch in diese Einsamkeit.[10]

(Refuge)

(It is so still; the heath basks in the warm rays of the midday sun, a
rose-red hue hovers about its ancient graves; the heather is in bloom;
its scent is rising to the blue summer sky.

Beetles clad in golden armor scurry through the bush, the bees are
clinging, stem by stem, to the heather's blossoms, the birds are whiz-
zing from the heather—the air is filled with the sound of larks.

A ramshackle house stands lonely here and sundrenched; the beekeeper is leaning out the door, snugly gazing at his bees; his boy is
sitting on a rock nearby carving pipes from Spanish reed.

A stroke of the distant village clock barely stirs the noontime rest;
the old man's lids now shut, he is dreaming of his harvests of honey.
—Not a sound of the turbulent times has ever penetrated this solitude.)

As in most of Storm's works, the motif of reminiscence, though
well concealed here, is the central element largely determining
the formal characteristics of many poems and novellas. Reminiscence was Storm's means of escaping from a meaningless, un-
promising present. The poet's reminiscent perspective is hidden
behind an apparent objective description of a place and a point in
time. The time is the present, the noon hour. The timelessness of
the idyllic scene signifies a complete surrender to nature, which is
to give permanence to this moment.[11] Strangely, however, the very
realistic setting and objective attitude implicit in the description
of this "refuge" is cast in doubt by the final two verses of the poem
which represent a break with the idyllic atmosphere of the poem
(the dash indicates that the poet had felt this himself): "—Not a
sound of the turbulent times has ever penetrated this solitude."
The individual phenomena in which permanence is sought (the
heath, the warm sunlight, the beekeeper) as well as the moment
(the walk, the hour) cannot really conceal the poet's concern
about a turbulent present. The dreamlike quality, the unreality of
a mirage attaching to the first three stanzas are identified as an
"interior" event—as something in the poet's mind. The stroke of
the clock may be distant and barely audible, the beekeeper may be
dreaming, but these very references cast doubt upon the objective
perspective of the poet who seems to be secure (but isn't) in the
belief of having transcended the limits of space and time. Actually, the structure of the poem is determined by the motif of reminiscence which is represented here by a personal or subjective
attitude (a feeling of transiency and the escape from it by recalling the idyl), implying that reality can be known only through
personal experience. It is, thus, a poem of an intense inward experience, its formal aspects of objectivity (the present tense, the
descriptive style) notwithstanding. According to Spycher, the
concluding two verses of the last stanza provide the clue for the
organizational principle of the poem (corroborating our own
analysis): the flight from the turmoil of the times (though un-
stated) forms the poem's beginning, the description of the idyl its

middle, and the return to the turmoil (as the inevitable conclusion) its ending.[12]
Structurally quite similar is the elegiac cycle "Constanze," written in 1871, six years after her death:

Constanze

1

Längst in das sichere Land der Vergangenheit warst du
    geschieden;
Nun, wie so viele zuvor, dämmerte wieder ein Tag.
Laut schon sangen die Schwalben; da neben mir krachte das
    Bettchen,
Und aus dem rosigen Schlaf hob sich ein Köpfchen empor.
"Ebbe!" so rief ich, "klein Ebbe!"—Da kniete sie schon in den
    Kissen;
Aber geheimnisvoll blickten die Augen mich an.
"Ebbe?" frug sie zurück, und leis aus innerstem Herzen
Klang's wie ein Lachen herauf: "Elschen hiess ich ja sonst!
Wer doch nannte mich Elschen?" Da plötzlich fiel es wie Schatten
Über das Kindergesicht; trüb sich umflorte das Aug.
"Ja, wer nannte dich so?"—Und zögernd kamen die Worte:
"Meine Mutter." Und still senkte das Köpfchen sich nun.
Lange kniete sie so. Den sterblichen Augen unfassbar—
War sie dem Kinde genaht, die mich so lange beglückt?

2

Nicht dem Geliebten allein; wie vielen wardst du entrissen!
Glaubten die Freunde doch kaum, ohne dich blühe die Welt.
Deine geliebten Rosen, nur dreimal blühten sie wieder,
Und deinen Namen wie lang hab ich von keinem gehört.
Rastlos wandert die Zeit, in den Augen der Kinder, verdämmert
Mählich dein Bild, und bald—wer noch wüsste von dir!
Denn so schwindet der Menschen Gedächtnis: Siehe, noch
    einmal,
Höher als je zuvor, hebt es die spiegelnde Flut;
Scheidender Abendstrahl der Sonne verklärt es noch einmal;
Doch wie die Welle verrauscht, nimmt und begräbt es die
    Nacht.[13]

1

(You had long since passed into the safe realm of the past; Now another day was to dawn as so many before it. Already the swallows were chirping noisily, when next to me the small bed creaked, and a small head rose from blissful slumber. "Ebbe," I called, "little Ebbe!" —She was already kneeling on the pillows. Her eyes looked at me mysteriously. "Ebbe?" she replied, and softly from the depths of her heart it sounded like laughter: "Elschen used to be my name! Who would call me Elschen?" Suddenly, as if it were a shadow, the child's face changed; the eye welled up, darkly. "Yes, who would call you thus?" And hesitatingly she spoke the words: "My mother." And silently she bowed her head. And so she knelt for a long time. Incomprehensible to mortal eyes—. Had she approached the child who had made me happy for so long?

2

Not only to your beloved but to so many people you were lost! Your friends could hardly believe that the world would flourish without you.—Your beloved roses have bloomed barely three times, and your name how long since I have heard it spoken by anyone. Relentlessly, time moves on; in the eyes of the children your image is slowly fading away, and soon—who would remember you! For this is how human memory fades: Behold, once more, higher than ever before the glassy tide lifts it up; the waning rays of the setting sun transfigure it once more; but as the wave dies away, the night takes it away and buries it.)

Storm's inclination was toward the simple folk-song strophe and its iambic or trochaic meter. The classical elegiac meter here, obviously, is to lend dignity to the cycle, as well as conforming to its epic and epitaphlike character. On the other hand, the elegy's very intimate character (the first canto tells of the child's awakening and recalling of her mother's death, and the second of the poet's sense of loss) does not seem too well suited for the stately habit of its distichs.

The structure of the poem is bipolar. The central motif is sounded in the opening verse of the first canto ("You had long since passed into the safe realm of the past") in an obvious allusion to Seneca's stoicism. The opposing motif is stated in the second canto with the disquieting realization that even the past is not safe, because as memory fades with time so does the past.

As with other poems already referred to, the descriptive style is disrupted by a (barely concealed) personal reflection contained in the question: "Had she approached the child who had made me happy for so long?" This becomes even clearer if we consider the original version of the last four verses.[14] Here the departed and almost forgotten mother approaches her child for the last time in a supernatural reunion. Storm himself must have felt the complete break this represents with the simple epic style, since he changed it to a question in the later version, thus interrupting his narrative with a speculation. Finally, there is the same tendency toward the supernatural (which also figures prominently in his prose) as the only possible means of perpetuating the moment beyond itself—even beyond the "safe realm of the past" (beyond Seneca's stoic statement) toward the "infinite poem," as Manfred Hausmann once called it.[15]

Another aspect of Storm's striving for objectivity is his aim, already noted in the Constanze elegy, to expurgate any specific historical references in order to achieve universality. The extant variants of his poems corroborate that intention. The recently discovered manuscript of his patriotic poem "Gräber an der Küste" (Graves on the Coast) (1850), probably the orginal version,[16] shows, in comparison with the subsequent versions, Storm's efforts to eliminate specific references to the historical event. The occasion for the poem was the defeat of the Prussians who, after an unsuccessful siege, tried to liberate Friedrichstadt on the North Sea from Danish occupation. Thus, stanza six was omitted from the final version:

> Unwillig muss die wilde Dannbrog
> An eurer Gruft das Ehrenamt verwalten;
> Ihr zwangt den Feind, der euch hinunterzog,
> Sein Banner bei den Todten zu entfalten.

(Unwillingly the wild Danish flag must be the guard of honor at your tomb; you forced the enemy who dragged you down to unfurl his banner among the dead.)

Similarly, Bernd shows how the last verse of the ninth stanza was changed for the sake of a more general meaning: "Doch habt ihr sie [die Heimat] vor Deutschlands Schmach gerettet" (But you saved [our homeland] from Germany's humiliation) became "Doch habt ihr sterbend sie vor Schmach gerettet" (Yet, dying, you saved it from humiliation).

This process of "purification," of course, relates directly to Storm's lyrical canon of the immediate experience which lies in the "soul" of the poem, in its naturalness. To Storm, it means attention to the lyrical elements of sound and internal form as against mere prosodic considerations. In "Graves on the Coast," the "timeless" experience of the violation of one's humanity by the invaders takes precedence over the original issue of the Dano-Prussian war. The illumination of the condition interests Storm, for whom the historical event is merely a catalyst. Moreover, to Storm, it is the eternal value of inviolate feeling which gives meaning to life beyond the ravishes of time and death. Such a meaning he could find only in the individual experience. But not in a vision of a total philosophical concept.

Quite similarly, in another poem dealing with the Danish invasion of Schleswig-Holstein ("Im Herbste 1850") (In the Autumn of 1850), Storm keeps the references to the specific situation to a minimum; he hints at the real but elusive meaning in a letter to his revered poetic mentor and friend, Eduard Mörike: "The poem originated as the immediate expression of a violated patriotic feeling [Heimatgefühl] in the fall of 1850 when here, at the cemetery [in Husum], the wreaths and flags of our Schleswig-Holstein soldiers were removed [by the Danes]." [17] Storm's political lyric and the proverbs of his later years (from his voluntary exile in Heiligenstadt and after his return to Husum in 1865) reveal his resentment, and even hatred, for Prussian officialdom, the aristocracy, organized religion, and the Danish government.

His political and proverbial or philosophical poetry has two recurring motifs as its core: the *carpe diem* motif and the motif of personal integrity and loyalty in the face of great adversity. What is, therefore, more nearly the expression of personal suffering appears in the guise of an objective norm, the fact of man's duty to moral behavior, to an affirmation of life, although there may be no meaning to life after death. The last part of the eighth canto of the cycle "Tiefe Schatten" (Dark Shadows) (1865), which Storm had withheld from publication during his lifetime, extols a purely esthetic view of life:

> Aus dem seligen Glauben des Kreuzes
> Bricht ein andrer hervor,
> Selbstloser und grösser.
> Dessen Gebot wird sein:
> Edel lebe und schön,

Ohne Hoffnung künftigen Seins
Und ohne Vergeltung,
Nur um der Schönheit des Lebens willen.[18]

(From the blessed faith in the cross another breaks forth, less selfish and greater. Its commandment will be: Live nobly and beautifully, without hope in a future existence and without retribution, solely for the sake of life's beauty.)

"Nur heute ist" (1873) invokes the *carpe diem* motif—one of the major motifs in Storm's poetry—in answer to the same fear of death and ultimate oblivion:

Nur heute ist, und morgen ist zu spät!
hast du ein Weib, so nimm sie in den Arm
Und hauch's ihr ein, dass sie es auch versteht.

Fällt auf ihr Antlitz dann des Abgrunds Schein,
Der heut noch oder morgen euch begräbt,
Getrost! nur um so schöner wird sie sein.

Und bebt ihr Herz, dann halte sie so fest,
Dass ihr zusammen in die Tiefe stürzt.
Was wollt ihr mehr!—Und Schweigen ist der Rest.[19]

(There is only today, and tomorrow is too late! If you have a wife, take her into your arms and whisper it to her, so she will understand.
If then the shadow of the abyss falls upon her face, which will bury you today or tomorrow, feat not! for she will be so much more beautiful.
And if her heart trembles, hold her so fast that you plunge into the depth together. What more can you ask! And the rest is silence.)

A typical expression of the Stormian motif of integrity and loyalty can be found in the political (i.e., anti-Danish) poem "Die fremde Sprache" (The Foreign Language) (1863). The preservation of one's roots and one's national identity is an ethical and, more important, an existential imperative:

Die fremde Sprache schleicht von Haus zu Haus,
Und deutsches Wort und deutsches Lied löscht aus;
Trotz alledem—es muss beim alten bleiben:
Die Feinde handeln, und die Freunde schreiben.[20]

(The foreign tongue sneaks from house to house, and German word
and German song expires; still—things do not change: our foes act
and our friends write.)

Another instance of Storm's desire for objectivity is his frequent
change of title for his poems. For example, the relatively late
poem "Geh nicht hinein" (Do not Enter) (1879) was first published under the title "To a Dead Man" occasioned by the impression which the death of young Count Reventlow, the son of his
friend, had made on the poet. In a letter to Gottfried Keller,
Storm stressed how he had meant to convey the impression made
by the sight of a dead person on anyone, thus treating the specific
occasion which prompted the poem as purely accidental.[21] If the
point of Storm's endeavor to "objectify" the personal and specific
experience needed further elaboration, "Welt-Lauf" (The Way of
the World) (1867) would serve that purpose well. In this epi-
gram, Storm again turns the personal and disagreeable experience
of life under Prussian rule[22] into the universal theme of "the way
of the world," a threat to personal integrity. Moreover, Prussian
bureaucracy and authoritarianism and his new role as an official
of that government had disillusioned him completely, and he regarded the Prussians with no more sympathy than the Danes:

> Wer der Gewalt genüber steht
> In Sorgen für der Liebsten Leben,
> Der wird zuletzt von seinem Ich
> Ein Teil und noch ein Teilchen geben.
> Und dürstet er nach reinster Luft,
> Er wird zuletzt ein halber Schuft.[23]

(He who confronts power with concern for the lives of his loved
ones, will, in the end, give of himself a small part and still another.
And although he may desire the purest air, he will finally be half a
scoundrel.)

III *The Tradition of the Lied*

The historical explanation for the inwardness and idyllic character of much of Storm's poetry must be sought in the post-
Goethean disillusionment with idealism; hence, Storm's tenet that
the art of poetry consists of giving expression to a general concept
through an individual experience.[24]

Although it is merely an uneasy feeling in Storm, the fact that only an individual truth is known finds its expression in an "objective" stance, which is never more than a struggle to maintain a philosophical attitude of courage in the face of a meaningless existence. As has been observed by one critic, philosophically and intellectually, the "realists" of Storm's time have very little to say, since their ideas do not exceed the level of mere opinion. While realism contributed much to form, it remained impoverished intellectually. This is one of the reasons for the strong countermoves prefigured in Friedrich Hebbel, C. F. Meyer, and Friedrich Nietzsche.[25] It is, therefore, only natural that Storm preferred the folksong mode or, generally, the German form of the *Lied* for his poetry, since this tradition represents the fusion of the subject with the object, or of the self with the world. Storm called himself the "last lyric poet," because he regarded himself as the last representative of a tradition which began with Johann Christian Günther and the poets of the "Storm and Stress." The form of the *Lied* flourished during the Romantic period and was once more revived, in a period of intellectual transition, by Heine, Eichendorff, Mörike, and Storm. In Storm, however, the characteristic fusion lacks the Romantic striving for, and belief in, a total harmonious universe with the *Lied* celebrating the ultimate union of the self with the nonself. The total objectivity which comes with a unifying cosmology is now merely a lost ideal which he seeks to recover.

Perhaps, in an attempt to preserve an order inwardly which could no longer be maintained outwardly, Storm clung to what he could actually cope with: the individual phenomenon. As Johannes Klein has remarked about the poetic realists, "it is the locale of landscape which is also the locale of history. The realities of social and historical life are bound up with the landscape, and the homeland is an antidote to restlessness, rootlessness, and the vagaries of human fate." [26] Specifically, Husum, which Storm immortalized in the poem "Die Stadt" (1851), is the external boundary for internal freedom, within which he was able to create the typical fates and characters which symbolize mankind, or, as he wrote to his young admirer, the poetess Hermione von Preuschen, "I would wish very much, for your own sake, that your unnatural urge for travel be satisfied. You will then learn, I hope, that, essentially, the world in which one lives exists within oneself." [27] This attitude of withdrawal from "the marketplace," as it were, is significant, because it denotes, among other things, that Storm felt he had, ultimately, only himself to rely on. In this connection, his frequently quoted statement about classicism is important, because of what it implies for the limitations upon his insights into the world and himself. He once observed that if a poet could lay claim to being a classic, he could do so only if "his works reflected the essence of his time in artistically perfect form" and that, therefore, "he himself [Storm], would have to be content with a place on the sidelines." [28] It is precisely because Storm's oeuvre lacks any genuinely normative aspect (except a historical nexus, i.e., one of continuity, or, as in some of his novellas, an ethical nexus), that is, a nonhistorical and nonmoral, unified cosmology indispensable to an exemplary, or classical style, that Storm's statement is so revealing. It not only betrays a misconception of what is classical but also confirms the defensive and subjective nature of his lyric poetry and prose. Moreover, his self-appraisal reflects a dilemma which obtained not only in his case, but in that of his contemporaries as well, namely that the creation of a classical literature would have been quite impossible in Storm's time, given its cultural ambience and painful awareness of a fragmented, meaningless reality.

It is perhaps not saying too much if one defines Storm's lyrical theory and practice as a kind of esthetic bastion against the dissolution of the patriarchal and idyllic life, although its poetic expression is almost always found by indirection, through a dark premonition that things have changed irrevocably. Hence, he was time and again moved to stipulate the pure lyric ("Naturlaut") as the chief criterion for the quality of a poem. It is the quintessential character of a phenomenon that Storm, not unlike Rilke in his "Dinggedichte," wishes to make known. The careful and extreme concentration which this goal requires is expressed in the strong emotional content of his poems, through the intensity of the private experience. Storm not only tried, but fully succeeded in creating the careful balance between rhythm and sound, the "movement of the heart," as he called it. This unmistakable musical quality of his love and nature poems to this day has attracted the best among German composers (e.g., Johannes Brahms, Hugo Wolf, Alban Berg) to set them to music.[29] The "organic" relationship between content and form was the ultimate touchstone of a poem's worth for Storm and furnished the proper perspective for its "musicality." Indicative of this demand was Storm's attitude toward Emanuel Geibel, the poet laureate of Wilhelmian Germany, and, according to Storm himself, his esthetic opposite. In the following quatrain (1885) addressed to Geibel, Storm makes his position clear:

> Poeta laureatus: Es sei die Form ein Goldgefäss,
> In das man goldnen Inhalt giesst.
> Ein anderer: Die Form ist nichts als der Kontur,
> Der den lebendigen Leib beschliesst.[30]

(Poeta laureatus: Let the form be a golden vessel into which golden content is poured.
Another poet: The form is nothing but the contour which surrounds the living body.)

These verses not only betray Storm's clear rejection of poetry as mere formalism, they also constitute a refusal to accept certain political realities of his time. Geibel was the official bard of the Hohenzollern dynasty, and, in Storm's opinion, he was degrading his artistic talents by singing the praises of his emperor and Reich. When, on the occasion of a party given in honor of Storm's seventieth birthday, one of the guests proposed a toast to the emperor, Storm replied with a polemic thrust against Geibel, without ever mentioning his name. Geibel's fame eclipsed that of any other living poet in the country, and this, in part, was made possible by the literary historians and critics of the time who praised him lavishly against their better judgment. Storm's attitude toward Bismarck's robber-baron politics ("Räuberpolitik") and Prussian Junkerdom was well known to his friends. On that day he simply attacked the regime through one of its quasi-official exponents.[31] Incidents of this kind would tend to explain the idyllic nature of Storm's art as a refuge from unpleasant political and social facts.

A rather typical example for Storm's folksong-style poetry is "Im Walde" (In the Forest) (1849).

> Hier an der Bergeshalde
> Verstummet ganz der Wind;
> Die Zweige hängen nieder,
> Darunter sitzt das Kind.

Sie sitzt in Thymiane,
Sie sitzt in lauter Duft;
Die blauen Fliegen summen
Und blitzen durch die Luft.

Es steht der Wald so schweigend,
Sie schaut so klug darein;
Um ihre braunen Locken
Hinfliesst der Sonnenschein.

Der Kuckuck lacht von ferne,
Es geht mir durch den Sinn:
Sie hat die goldnen Augen
Der Waldeskönigin.[32]

(Here, at the foot of the mountain, the wind is dying down completely; the branches are hanging low, and the child is sitting underneath.

She is sitting in the thyme, she is sitting in pure fragrance; the blue flies are humming and flashing through the air.

The forest is so still, and she looks so bright; sunshine flows about the brown curls of her hair.

The cuckoo is laughing in the distance. It occurs to me: She has the golden eyes of the forest queen.)

This poem is almost pure magic. Its effect is entirely upon the senses of hearing, seeing, and smelling (the fragrance of the thyme, the humming flies, the golden eyes, and so on). The simple main clauses (there are no dependent clauses), the choice of simple words, and the gentle flow of the iambic meter underscore the naïve and magic quality of this *Lied*. The child (actually, Elisabeth, the girl portrayed in the novella *Immensee*) is the forest queen, because the poet's vision—the transformation of the child—arises from the enchantment of this scene.

Even in Storm's political and epigrammatic poems the stress is upon the lament. The poet sought refuge in the art of the *Lied* and the folk song which, originally, (in the Romantic tradition) signified an affirmation of life and its universal harmony. This harmony is anxiously sought by Storm, but is, in the end, unattainable for him, because of his acute awareness of the transitoriness of life and the ultimate power of death. In this sense, as has justly been observed by many critics, Storm is the last of the purely lyrical poets belonging to a tradition which began with Christian Günther in the early eighteenth century.

Instinctively, Storm sought refuge in the social certitudes of a patriarchal past. He considered himself the last representative of one of Husum's old families. Inevitably, this led to a kind of estheticism in his poetry whereby the idyllic mood or the painful echo of a happier, though never experienced, past had to compensate for the simple verities which once provided the solid ground for the inwardness and intensity ("Innigkeit") of the venerable German *Lied*. To restate what is, indeed, a very essential point: apart from one lyrical cycle, two poems that are almost modern in their proselike paratactical style and their free rhythms ("Geh') nicht hinein"; "Ein Sterbender"), the epigrams, two ritornelli, a ghasel, and an elegy, it is the *Lied* with its simple folk-song stanza which triumphs in Storm's work. The complex form of the sonnet, for example, was attempted by him only once ("Neuer Frühling" [New Spring]), which is not surprising given its strict form and antithetical structure.

IV   *The Idyl and Politics*

In Storm's anthology of German poetry since Claudius (*Hausbuch aus deutschen Dichtern seit Claudius*, 1870), the criteria for the inclusion of a poem culminate in "inwardness,"—"listening," "feeling," "seeing" all at once. And as if that were not enough, Storm tells the reader in the foreword that one merit of his anthology lies in what has been omitted from it. Of course, the omitted genres comprise practically everything except the *Lied*. Even the "intellectual or reflective lyric" ("Gedankenlyrik") is excluded from this confessional anthology, where Goethe must take second place behind Friedrich Rückert, Heine, and Eichendorff if one merely considers the number of poems by which each author is represented. This self-imposed limitation, which is nevertheless impressive in the conviction it carries, frequently compelled Storm to defend his position vis-à-vis his friends and fellow poets. The relevant correspondence with Paul Heyse, the later winner of the Nobel Prize for literature and literary star of Storm's age, frequently refers to Storm's exclusive lyrical canon. Gottfried Keller, Storm's famous Swiss contemporary, once referred to this intransigence in lyrical matters with his customary gentle irony: "I am very much looking forward to your new verses and shall look at the same with listening eyes and listen to them with seeing ears." [33]

In spite of this problematic situation, Storm was able to create a body of lyrical poetry which, as all genuine lyric, is profoundly moving precisely because of its private, intimate character. For him, the lyrical mode was a release from the deeply perturbing uncertainties of life in all its aspects. The untimely patriarchal and patrician values to which Storm adhered in his poetry prompted him to refer to himself as a poet "of the old school." It was more than unfair of Rudolf Gottschall, the most influential literary critic of the time in Germany, to accuse Storm of being a sentimental poet far removed from the problems of his time. He called him a representative "of a literary rearguard which tries to cover the retreat of beaten Romanticism." [34] It must be remembered, of course, that Gottschall's criticism was leveled a few years after the abortive revolution of 1848 which, as it turned out, destroyed the only opportunity for Germany, in that century, to catch up with the French Revolution in ridding itself of the vestiges of its powerful landed aristocracy and regional absolutism. Gottschall, as the unofficial literary critic of the Hohenzollern Empire, opened his devastating critique of Storm's poetry with the remark "No sooner has the scarlet fever of the blood-red lyric of liberation subsided than the German muse begins to come down with the evil smallpox of sentimentality and wild fantasy." [35] This polemic against Storm appeared in 1853, the same year in which Fontane published a review of *Immensee*, we do not know whether by accident or design; but, in any case, it did set matters right again. Fontane immediately perceived the profundity and inwardness of Storm's poetry and recognized in him a genuine poetic talent.

Aside from that, however, it is fairly obvious that Storm and the contemporary writers in Germany could be accused of failing to take a positive stand in matters of political and social concern, although hardly in the sense which Gottschall implied. The very fact of Germany's social and political backwardness and isolation —in contrast to its scientific and economic progress—caused the best among its poets and writers to "withdraw from the market-place," as it were, and to adhere to values which, to Storm at least, were far superior to what Prussia might place as a model before a divided nation. The only real defense against the charge of a parochialism in Storm's writings rests with the universal character of their language and their human appeal (unlike the regional dialect literature produced by Fritz Reuter and Klaus Groth, who are not characteristic authors of their period). It is for this reason, too, that Storm wrote only three poems in his native Low German dialect, which was the language spoken at his home. Moreover, the best among Storm's poems reveal his struggle with a reality he saw as being in conflict with his inner needs. Hence, the patriarchal values of home, a strict but benevolent order, an all-encompassing love of life, family, and nature dominate the thematic range of his lyric poetry. It is for the same reasons that his political poems almost exclusively represent the reaction to events that threatened his own well-being which, in turn, depended fundamentally on the safety and security of the "fatherland" (meaning to Storm only Schleswig-Holstein) and his family. As has been noted before, Storm's political views coincided with the historically evolved form of government in the duchies of Schleswig and Holstein, where the people had always been represented by the social estates. Thus, in spite of Storm's hatred of the aristocracy and petty officialdom, he was at heart a monarchist.[36] His criticism always turned against the inhuman and exceedingly petty side of the ruling classes, including the clergy. Storm was in favor of German unification but more in the sense of a cultural and intellectual union than of a political power. Hence, his rapid disillusionment with Prussia after its annexation of the duchies in 1867 and their liberation from Danish rule in 1864. In that year, after his return to Husum from voluntary exile in Potsdam and Heiligenstadt, Storm revealed his essentially apolitical nature:

> Wir können auch die Trompete blasen
> Und schmettern weithin durch das Land;
> Doch schreiten wir lieber in Maientagen,
> Wenn die Primeln blühn und die Drosseln schlagen,
> Still sinnend an des Baches Rand.[37]

(We too can sound the herald and let it ring throughout the land; but in May, when the primrose blooms and the thrush is singing, we prefer —in quiet reflection—to stride to the edge of the brook.)

The conservatism suggested by these verses is offset, however, by Storm's vacillation between an attitude of resignation and impassioned dissatisfaction with the human condition. Or, expressed in terms of literary periodization, he vacillates between an attitude typical of the *Biedermeier* poets, on the one hand, and of the so-called realists on the other.

V *Biedermeier, Love, Marriage, and Family*

Jost Hermand's characterization of the Biedermeier period enables us to make a comparison of the similarities and differences in Storm's attitude toward the subject of love:

It was impossible for the *Biedermeier* poets to come to terms with the wealth of reality. There was no escaping the historical, social, and political realities of the present for them. . . . Therefore, the *Biedermeier* period, seeking peace with the scientific and historical realities, reverts to a static conservatism as a means of coming to grips with the totality of life. . . . Hence, certain absolutes were considered bedrock truths: continuity (tradition) and high personal moral standards, which, when not fulfilled, resulted in solitude rather than a compromise with the limits of existence. Therefore, certain fundamental impressions once received remain unalterable. For Grillparzer it is Kathi, for Mörike Peregrina, for Stifter Fanny, and for Droste it is her unhappy love for two men in her youth. These experiences were like an unsurmountable wall between them and their later experiences. The coexistence of marriage and eros which had prevailed from the *Minnesang* period to the Rococo is now replaced by the static concept of love as a singular and exclusive experience. If its fulfillment fails, only resignation or a conservative attitude of old age remains. This decadent internal climate was only destroyed by the realism which followed it. It broke with the moral and metaphysical exclusiveness of the restoration period, replacing it with pragmatic and dynamic attempts at coming to terms with life, once more affording openness and flexibility toward human existence.[38]

Storm's love-poetry which celebrates—much like that of the *Biedermeier* poets—the tranquillity and satisfaction of mutual possession and the happiness of his marriage, contrasts sharply with the passion and sensuousness of the love poems dedicated to Dorothea Jensen in "Mysterium" (Mystery) (written in 1848 but withheld from publication until after his death) and the cycle of six poems "Ein Buch der roten Rose" (A Book of the Red Rose) (1848). These intimate poems, prompted by the passionate love affair with Dorothea during the first two years of his marriage to

Constanze, represent a radical departure not only from the conservative *Biedermeier* morality of the 1830's and 1840's but also
from Storm's own period of sentimental *Goldschnittlyrik:*

> Hör mir nicht auf solch Geschwätze,
> Liebes Herz, dass wir Poeten
> Schon genug der Liebeslieder,
> Ja zuviel gedichtet hätten.
>
> Ach, es sind so kläglich wenig,
> Denn ich zählte sie im stillen,
> Kaum genug, dein Nadelbüchlein
> Schicklich damit anzufüllen.
>
> Lieder, die von Liebe reimen,
> Kommen Tag für Tage wieder;
> Doch wir zwei Verliebte sprechen:
> Das sind keine Liebeslieder.[39]

(Do not list to such chatter, my beloved, that we, the poets, have
made enough, indeed too many, songs of love.
Alas, there are so pitifully few, for I counted them quietly; there are
barely enough properly to fill the pages of your little journal.
Songs which rhyme of love come and go, day after day; but we
two lovers say: These are no songs of love.)

While Storm was a member of the "Tunnel Society" in Berlin,
he produced the poem "Geschwisterblut" (Incest) as an answer
to a similar theme treated in a poem by Kugler. The subsequent
controversy about his "ballada incestuosa," as Storm called it, led
him to define his views on art and morals. He wrote to his friend
and fellow member Friedrich Eggers that moral considerations in
the poem have significance only insofar as they are being overcome. The problem is with the subject of incest and not with its
treatment. Customs and manners have their basis in natural law.
If in an exceptional instance the incestuous urge exists, the moral
code is without foundation, and the individual may feel justified
in claiming for himself an exception. The existence of passion is its
own justification. The nub of the poem lies in the conflict of a
natural right with the accepted moral code, which is here boldly
violated by brother and sister after a vain effort to reconcile the
demands of nature and custom.[40]
Storm, who, because of the passionate side of his poetry, bore

the name *Tannhäuser* in the society, suffered intensely from his strong convictions regarding the sanctity of marriage, the absolute and exclusive demands of love as a personal and social responsibility (very much like the *Biedermeier* concept of it), and his own passionate nature. As a burgher and ethical being, he had to admit to immoral behavior, and because of his infidelity to Constanze he sought to give expression to his guilt feelings in the cycle "Weisse Rosen," (1851) describing the quiet suffering of the wife and the husband's remorse:

> Du gehst an meiner Seite hin
> Und achtest meiner nicht;
> Nun schmerzt mich deine weisse Hand,
> Dein süsses Angesicht.
>
> O sprich wie sonst ein liebes Wort,
> Ein einzig Wort mir zu!
> Die Wunden bluten heimlich fort,
> Auch du hast keine Ruh.
>
> Der Mund, der jetzt zu meiner Qual
> Sich stumm vor mir verschliesst,
> Ich hab ihn ja so tausendmal,
> Vieltausendmal geküsst.
>
> Was einst so überselig war,
> Bricht nun das Herz entzwei;
> Das Aug, das meine Seele trank,
> Sieht fremd an mir vorbei.[41]

(You are walking by my side and do not notice me; now it gives me pain to see your pale hand, your sweet face.

Oh speak to me a loving word as before, just one! The wounds bleed on in secret and you, too, are restless.

Your lips, which now are closed much to my sorrow, I have kissed them a thousand times, many thousand times.

What was once abundant bliss now tears the heart asunder; the eye, libation of my soul, looks past me, a stranger.)

Behind all this passion lies the fear of death and nothingness. Manfred Hausmann draws our attention to this existential aspect of Storm's love lyrics:

Storm knew that the real confrontation with the fact of death would result in increasing loneliness. Everybody is, in the last analysis—and when confronted with his own mortality—alone. The only defense is love. Love is, to Storm, the natural reaction of mortal man to his lonely fear of death. "Love is nothing but the fear of loneliness on the part of mortal man." Even if it is just love for the moment. With increasing awareness of transiency and death, Storm's desire and ability to love, and to be loved, grew. While many people push aside such thoughts and while Storm may have tried himself to do so, he never succeeded for long. He would have succumbed to despair if the embers of love had not, from time to time, banished the shadow of death. He opposed the absolute of death with the absolute of love.[42]

There is also the social aspect of the problem. The *Biedermeier* trait of absolute love, as it ought to be called, with its demand of unconditional surrender to the sanctity of matrimony, was very strong in Storm. The very central function of love in his thinking, its originally Romantic conception, its function as a refuge from chaos, drives Storm into a conflict beyond resolution. This conflict gave rise to a theme frequently treated in his novellas, namely that of love as a spiritual and physical inclination and the austere concept of love as a social obligation. The earliest treatment of this theme is found in the poem "Hyazinthen" (Hyacinths) (1852) (much admired by Thomas Mann for its similarity to his own treatment of the dualism of art and life) where the beloved must "dance" for the world and its demands of propriety. The poet sees her passing, her feet in the air, held by indifferent arms. The hyacinths exude their sensuous aroma in the night, the candles are burning, the violins are screaming, and the rows of couples open and close. Each stanza ends with the refrain "I would like to sleep, but you must dance."[43] Jealousy, sultriness, and resignation engender the atmosphere of this poem.

It is, indeed, a Romantic urge that prompts Storm to seek an ultimate union of souls beyond all earthbound limitations. His natural inclination contradicts, however, his belief in the material basis of all life. Two years before her death, he wrote to his wife: "You know that I believe death to be the ultimate end of the individual. In spite of this, I have the desire to make ready for a flight beyond this boundary into the unknown and boundless, to be tied to a soul which is prepared to share with me everything to the ultimate bounds of existence."[44] The self, in fact, quite literally the material self, stands in the way of a perfect union that he so much desired:

But . . . have you [Constanze] ever thought of it? Even in close proximity we have never more than our own concept of each other, the image we abstract for ourselves! But we never have ourselves; unless the body be also the soul; and even when we embrace in deepest love, I am compelled to see you as a mystery which I am unable to solve.[45]

The realization of this ultimate, insuperable separation of two beings is not only the recurrence of a Romantic problem in Storm, but also the product of his materialistic philosophy, which leads him beyond the *Biedermeier* attitude vis-à-vis marriage as a moral obligation. Because of Storm's complete adherence to Ludwig Feuerbach's materialistic and atheistic views ("the secular family has been unmasked as the secret of the holy family"),[46] Storm is led from his austere concept of marriage to a concept based upon a purely esthetic view of life, most notably in the eighth canto of the cycle "Dark Shadows," discussed earlier, and in some of the novellas dealing with the problem of marriage.

Perhaps the most profound meaning of love to Storm was its metaphysical possibility, as a hope against hope, not unlike the role of the supernatural in his poetry and prose. Reality, or the universe, is to Storm a chaotic concept, and the warmth of love and family offers the only possibility of a symbolic meaning to life, otherwise seen as a perpetual cycle of becoming and decaying:

Wie wenn das Leben wär nichts andres
Als das Verbrennen eines Lichts!
Verloren geht kein einzig Teilchen,
Jedoch wir selber gehn ins Nichts!

Denn was wir Leib und Seele nennen,
So fest in eins gestaltet kaum,
Es löst sich auf in Tausendteilchen
Und wimmelt durch den öden Raum.

Es waltet stets dasselbe Leben,
Natur geht ihren ew'gen Lauf;
In tausend neuerschaffnen Wesen
Stehn diese tausend Teilchen auf.

> Das Wesen aber ist verloren,
> Das nur durch ihren Bund bestand,
> Wenn nicht der Zufall die verstäubten
> Aufs neu zu einem Sein verband.[47]

(What if life were nothing but the burning of a candle! No single particle is lost yet we ourselves drift toward nothingness!

For what we call body and soul is not as one forever, disintegrating into a thousand parts all drifting through the void.

Life is forever the same, nature pursuing its eternal course; in a thousand new-born beings these thousand particles arise.

But their essence is forever lost, having existed only through their bond, unless mere chance binds them together once more to create a new being.)

These verses are prefaced by Friedrich Hebbel's lines: "Natur, du kannst mich nicht vernichten, / Weil es dich selbst vernichten heisst" (Nature, you cannot annihilate me, for that would mean annihilating yourself). Storm's own lines, quoted above, provide a telling answer, indeed.

In this context of an almost total dependence on a rather simplistic philosophy of materialism, Storm's incapacity as a thinker becomes obvious, and even more so his personal suffering growing out of the desperate need for a meaningful reality in the face of a nihilistic cosmology.[48] It is, therefore, more than a sentimental touch when Storm never tires of discussing his family problems and joys in his letters, poems, and, indirectly, in his novellas. In general, he perceives in the child and in the woman an instinctive accord with nature that is forever lost to the self-conscious male adult. It is an important factor when one considers Storm's almost religious cultivation of family relationships where no member of the close and distant family was unimportant.

Christmas was the most significant time of year in Storm's family, not because of its religious meaning, but because it provided the close union of the entire clan under the Christmas tree with its "magic bough" ("Märchenzweig") of which Storm spoke often. Storm's deep attachment to his family is particularly evident in those poems he addressed to his children and to the Christmas season in general. These poems show a sense of humor otherwise rare in his production. "Von Katzen" (Of Cats) (1849), for example, describes the idyl and delight of the Storm household populated by several generations of cats, the cook who wants to drown them, and the poet whose "humane" instincts conflict with the necessity of ridding the house of fifty-six cats. "Knecht Ruprecht" (1862), to cite another prominent example, has been memorized by generations of German schoolchildren. Originally it was written in dialogue. It describes what was undoubtedly the Christmas scene in Storm's family, the father talking to Ruprecht about his children, who have all been virtuous, diligently obeying the commands of parents and teachers during the year and who are, therefore, deserving of all the wondrous things which the "Christ Child" has brought them.

It is perhaps no accident that Eduard Mörike, the *Biedermeier* poet part excellence, was particularly taken with Storm's children's and Christmas poems, all of which exude the warmth and happiness of a closely knit family life, while the poet looks on good-naturedly and with satisfaction. Invariably, it was the naïve yet highly differentiated and deeply moving experiences of nature and family life in Storm's poetry which touched subsequent generations of poets. Not surprisingly, many contemporary poets have expressed their deep attachment to the peculiar atmosphere of intensity and "inwardness" characterizing much of Storm's poetry and recalling nostalgic sentiments of youth and home. Such significant but diverse poets and writers as Hugo von Hofmannsthal, Eduard von Keyserling, Hermann Hesse, Thomas Mann, Karl Krolow, and Manfred Hausmann have all, at different times and varying length, paid homage to Storm's lyrical genius.

VI *The Last Phase*

As we have seen, the years from 1852 until 1854 were the most significant ones for Storm's lyrical output. Yet among the most deeply moving are the poems which mark the last phase of his poetic production from 1867 to 1886. All of these were written after Constanze's death, the most shattering experience in Storm's life: "Tiefe Schatten" (1867), "Constanze" (1870), "Begrabe nur dein Liebstes" (1873), and the well-known poem "Über die Heide" (Across the Heath) (1875) recalling Constanze's death. The latter poem was composed, as Storm himself reports, during a walk across the heath near Constanze's birthplace. These couplets stand in poignant contrast to the exuberant lines of "Auf dem Segeberg" (1848–52) which celebrated Constanze's native region and the

complete happiness of the couple and their two young children—
"The world, the world, oh how it's smiling!" [49] Now the poet is
moved to ask if there has ever been a happy time in his life:

> Über die Heide hallet mein Schritt;
> Dumpf aus der Erde wandert es mit.
>
> Herbst ist gekommen, Frühling ist weit—
> Gab es denn einmal selige Zeit?
>
> Brauende Nebel geisten umher;
> Schwarz ist das Kraut und der Himmel so leer.
>
> Wär ich hier nur nicht gegangen im Mai!
> Leben und Liebe—wie flog es vorbei! [50]

(Across the heath sound my steps and muffled, from the earth, it is
wandering along.
  Autumn has come, spring is far—was there ever a time of bliss?
  Swirling mists are brewing; black is the heather and so empty the
sky.
  If only I had not walked here in May! Living and loving—how
quickly they passed!)

The poem fuses the memory of shared happiness with the
muffled echo from the steps on the ground, alluding to death as
the anonymous companion (*"it* wanders along") during the walk.
The dark quality of the vowels in "dumpf" (muffled) and "wandert" (wanders) further suggests the meaning for the "it" in "wandert es mit." In the last couplet, the open or high vowels in "wär"
(would be), "hier" (here), "im Mai" (in May), and the alliteration of the two nouns in the last verse ("Leben und Liebe") dis-
solve the act of recalling into almost pure sound, a soft lilt which
suggests the overpowering feeling of nostalgia for that moment of
happiness long past. The heavy stress on the opening and closing
syllables in every verse (the meter is dactylic-trochaic, the fourth
foot being catalectic throughout, accounting for the masculine
rhymes) provides the somber rhythm for the atmosphere of death
in the poem.
The poem's dualistic structure is apparent on several counts.
The alternation of back and front vowels in each couplet corresponds with a somber and brooding statement in every other line,
suggesting transiency and death. Further, there is a regular alter-

nation between an "above" and a "below." Each opening verse
refers to the locale of reminiscence, and each alternating line to
something below or far away, that is, to the past or to a strong
personal feeling: the muffled echo from below, the despair over
having never been happy, the blackness of the heather, and the
passage of love and life. The regular division of the poem into
rhyming pairs and, finally, the repetition of an alliterative pair in
verses one and eight ("*H*eide *h*allet"; "*L*eben und *L*iebe") confirm
the antithetical structure of this poem.

Although only two of the four concluding verses of each couplet
are actual long lines ("Langzeilen"), their rhythm causes them to
be read with a pause in each line, as if they were syntactically
separate as well, that is, as if, too, they consisted of two short lines
("Kurzzeilen"). Because of the dark vowels and the meaning of
the words, the heavy stress upon the syllables in lines two and
four causes a rhythmical break in the line which neither meter
nor syntax provide (". . . Erde—wandert; . . . einmal—selige
Zeit").

It is not difficult to see that this poem is not a moorland poem. It
is, rather, one of leave-taking, a final farewell to Constanze, ten
years after her death, a poem of almost pure sound and rhythm—
its dualistic structure of a desperate present and a subjective reaction to it notwithstanding—evoking a mood of death through the
much heavier beat and rhythmical spacing of the alternating lines,
contrasting with a faster pace or rhythm of each opening verse.
Thus, in spite of the poem's structure, it is not objective, because
of some inherent reflection or dialectic. It is completely subjective
in nature (though formally quite objective), and herein lies a
rather fundamental truth about Storm's poetry as a whole, namely
the cliché-like conventionality of his images and metaphors. The
cliché of the heath and the entirely evocative character of this
poem are further proof that the contrastive structure is merely the
"contour" of the "living body" (Storm) as will be remembered.
The objectivity is entirely contrived, hypostatized, providing a
realistic nexus of continuity (the reminiscent character of the
poem) for what is otherwise an entirely subjective process of recalling and feeling. The conventional images, therefore, serve to
amplify the atmosphere of transiency and despair, since the profound and essential rhythm is more important than the thought
content of the poem. The sentimental "so" in line six, which ren-

ders the image of the empty sky in purely emotional terms, shows quite clearly the subordination of thought to feeling and, at the same time, the problematic side of Storm's precept for the pure lyric, moving, as it must, on the borderline of sentimentality. Thus, cliché and experience (demanded by Storm) are perfectly blended, making it impossible to distinguish one from the other. The alliteration in "Leben und Liebe" and the reference to the month of May are as commonplace as spring and love. The "es" of line two, evoking the demonic and death, is another example of a conventional poetic association, namely that of the heath as the habitat of demons and ghosts. But, the heath itself, as a landscape, merely plays a mediating role, as the very personal point of departure for the poem (so necessary for Storm as a link with his own inner world, as we shall see in connection with his novellas) and an atmospheric prop.

To unite the most individual manner of representation with the most generally valid content was one of the key articles of Storm's lyrical faith. Yet, on the basis of our analysis it would appear that the reverse is true. Also, just as the heath in this poem serves as the personal point of departure, numerous other familiar localities in his novellas served a similar function, namely to justify—in an objective way—the entire effort of recalling or retelling in the first place. Images, then, quite generally function in Storm's poems as an impulse of experience, of "Anschaulichkeit" or concreteness; hence the limited inventory of his lyrical production where, for example, red roses stand for passion, white roses for the suffering it can cause, and the blanched hand or face or lips for quiet or suppressed sorrow. Storm was at an end point in the evolution of a lyrical style which had exhausted itself after the untrammeled expression of deeply moving private experiences (joyful or mournful) by Goethe, Matthias Claudius, and Eichendorff. It borders closely on the sentimental as is true of this and many other poems. It will be remembered that Storm described himself as a poet of the "old school," but, as with all who are born at the end of an important tradition, he could only seek out the unique, the particular and pretend that it still stood for the whole ("pars pro toto").

The brooding mood of the aging poet and a foreshadowing of death are present in this poem and the others of his last lyrical phase. In essence, his themes and motifs did not change. "Across

the Heath" with its motifs of reminiscence and the connection between nature and human fate harks back to "Abseits" (Refuge),
"Nur heute ist" (There Is Only Today) and many others. In this
respect, the period after 1867 offers mostly a repetition of the
motifs of his great period and his poetic preoccupation with the
death theme. For example, "Geh nicht hinein" (Do Not Enter)
(1879) conjures up the dreadful specter of physical death; "In
schwerer Krankheit" (Seriously Ill), written during Storm's illness
a year before his death, anticipates the ultimate end; and in "Es
ist ein Flüstern" (There Is a Whisper) (1872) a rapport with the
dead is sought.

In addition to some epigrams dedicated to persons close to him,
the last phase produced only one larger lyrical effort, called "Die
neuen Fiedellieder" (New Songs for the Fiddle) (1871), a cycle
of eleven songs. They represent the completion of Storm's earlier
poems by that title, going back to the time of the *Liederbuch,*
which was discussed at the beginning of the chapter. In style and
mood these convivial poems are artificial. They are more indebted
to Eichendorff's and Victor Scheffel's late and neo-Romantic poetry than they are to Storm's own lyrical genius. As Storm himself
admitted, "The 'Fiedellieder,' if at all, could only be continued in
the old mood which goes back to my student days when I was still
under Eichendorff's influence. . . ." [51] His effort to relive and re-
create the carefree mood of his youth was not successful, however. "They are the verses of an aging man who receives his
stimuli only from outside sources. Perhaps I shouldn't have had
them printed. . . ." [52]

During his entire life, Storm's poetic calling determined his
view of life. There was as yet no conflict between the burgher and
the artist which was to become so prominent in the works of
Thomas Mann. The themes of love and family, of fatherland and
native region, which are recurrently treated in the poems make it
clear that Storm's middle-class existence was to him inseparable
from his artistic persona. It is not so much the fact of a gradual
diminution of his lyrical production in his old age that characterizes this final phase; rather, it is the consistency of impetus and of
the self-imposed standards of absolute congruity between the private experience and its poetic form, as well as the illusion of objectivity to which he so often insisted adhering, which character-

ized his lyrics from the beginning and which caused the number of poems written toward the end to be relatively small.

As a final point, we are moved to ask what made Storm a poet. Perhaps another poet is best qualified to answer that question. By way of discussing Storm's selfish concept of love, Manfred Hausmann writes: "Perhaps this made him a poet in the first place: the conflict between the horror of death and passion, loneliness and euphoria, enjoyment of life and despair, finiteness and infinity, loyalty and treason, freedom and limitation; all of these created the conflicts necessary for his poetry." [53]

CHAPTER 3

Folklore and Fairy Tales

ALTHOUGH the number of original fairy tales or, more accurately, *Kunstmärchen* (literary fairy tales) written by Storm is only five, Storm's interest in these matters was considerable. His involvement with the genre dates from the 1840's and lasted throughout his life. Storm's keen interest in folklore and fairy tales makes him a direct descendant of the Romantic and *Biedermeier* traditions. He actively collected legends and folk tales from his native region of Schleswig-Holstein. He actually went to the sources in order to record the tales and legends orally transmitted.

During his years at the University of Kiel (1839–42), Storm, as we have previously mentioned, made the acquaintance of Theodor and Tycho Mommsen. In those days, the latter took a great interest in folklore, journalism, and politics. Storm, who was more of a follower than a leader in these activities, joined the brothers in their pursuits, contributing to Mommsen's newspaper *Schleswig-Holsteinische Zeitung* and keeping up a lively correspondence with Theodor Mommsen which eventually was to develop into friendship. Mommsen and Storm both contributed folklore material—which they had gathered jointly and separately—to Biernatzki's *Volksbuch für das Jahr 1844*. In the preface, Mommsen wrote: "When our plan becomes known to our countrymen, we hope to spark the same interest in others that heretofore has been demonstrated in our own circle, and we hope to establish contacts with any interested outsiders to gain their support for this patriotic undertaking which we have begun." [1]

The so-called *Döntjes* (amusing stories for children) which formed part of the Mommsen-Storm collection, Storm published two years later in his own name under the title *Geschichten aus der Tonne* (*Stories from the "Tonne"*). Another tale collected by Storm, *Das Märchen von den drei Spinnfrauen* (1843), was a new rendition of the Grimm fairy tale *Drei Spinnerinnen* (*Three Spin-ners*). The request for collaborators issued in Mommsen's preface produced a positive response from the well-known Germanist Karl Müllenhoff. Since Mommsen's interest in the collection began to wane after 1844, Storm also lost interest. Eventually, both turned over their material to Müllenhoff, who edited it as well as his own and published it in 1845 under the title of *Sagen, Märchen und Lieder der Herzogtümer Schleswig, Holstein und Lauenburg* (*Legends, Fairy Tales and Songs of the Duchies of Schleswig, Holstein, and Lauenburg*).

In connection with this aspect of Storm's literary life, it is inter-esting to note the explicit nationalism in the wording of Momm-sen's preface. These literary activities concern a time when the feelings for political and cultural independence from Denmark were running high in the three duchies. It was the time of Storm's emotional involvement with regional politics, and his first political poems were written then. Both Storm and Mommsen meant their native region when they spoke of their "countrymen," "patriot-ism," or—as Storm was wont to do—the "fatherland." In 1840, moreover, Danish had been introduced in northern Schleswig as the official language, thereby further alienating the German-speaking population and fanning political protest. These circum-stances, among others, lent to Mommsen's and Storm's seemingly harmless activity of collecting folklore a serious political motive, designed to assert the cultural heritage of the suppressed majority. In fact, the political and national awakening of Germany in the years immediately prior to 1848 had been greatly furthered by the struggle for independence of the Schleswig-Holsteiners.

I The Weird and Horrible

Beyond this political motivation, the source of Storm's activity and interest regarding folklore was quite personal, inspired by his immediate environment. As he wrote to Theodor Mommsen in 1842, "I was quite horror-struck at that point in my life [in his youth]; at home, in the evening, there used to be much discussion about legends and superstitious lore in general; a number of un-canny occurrences had happened to my mother in her last years which I had not known about previously . . ."; and often in the process "the poetic contemplation [of the uncanny] had to submit to a feeling of pure horror." [2] Indeed, the horrible and the uncanny had always struck a responsive note in Storm. His literary and his personal preoccupation with it lasted a lifetime. Aside from a collection of ghost stories (*Am Kamin,* 1861) (*By the Fireside*) and his fairy tales, numerous folk legends and motifs are incorporated in many of his otherwise "realistic" *novellas.* It was mostly the motif of the visionary that interested Storm and seems to constitute the common bond between the various superstitious lore and legends woven into the body of his prose. We are confirmed in this observation by Lee B. Jennings who finds, in fact, "that some of the symbols treated [of death, of the uncanny, and generally of the "dark side" of life] are not the result of purposeful deliberation about man's place in the cosmos but spring from deeper recesses of the mind. The grim and grisly material is, in fact, often set forth with such gusto that it seems to belie an origin in despondency. A part of Storm's mind relishes the horrible. . . . This fascination with the weird is not, in itself, to be labelled pessimistic." [3]

We have said that the visionary element figures prominently among the supernatural motifs in Storm's works. It is perhaps important here to correct the impression that, aside from the political significance of Storm's preoccupation with supernatural phenomena and other irrational ideas, the private aspect was decisive. In the recently published Mommsen-Storm correspondence (referred to previously) there are a number of references to these phenomena, which would indicate that Storm was by no means merely a passive recipient and transmitter of such lore. Rather, among the early letters addressed to his friend Mommsen we encounter theoretical statements about the genres of the folk legend and the fairy tale which demonstrate Storm's critical involvement as well. These letters also contain a hitherto unknown reference to the legend which was to be the seed from which grew his *magnum opus* and last novella (almost a novel, actually) *Der Schimmelreiter* (1888). The letter in question dates from February, 1843: "I told you once what it is like in the evening at our dikes and on the beach. I should say that whenever I had been there in the evening and alone I would be overcome by the presence of those uncanny figures who are fully embodied in the dike and beach legends which are so absolutely uncanny for me. The 'Schimmelreiter' [white horseman], no matter how fitting for this purpose [the Müllenhoff collection of regional tales and legends] by virtue of its overall character and as a dike legend, unfortunately does not belong to our fatherland." [4] This last reference to the "fatherland," by the way, must strike even the most objective reader as somewhat absurd, considering that the legend originated in the Duchy of Lauenburg on the Elbe which, after all, was politically and geographically allied with Schleswig-Holstein under Danish rule; but as a North Frisian Storm was unable to regard as his country a place beyond the boundaries of Schleswig-Holstein.

The spooky occurrences in the *Schimmelreiter* novellas are not confined to some ignorant villagers. One of the main characters, Hauke Haien's wife Elke, is endowed with a visionary gift. To be sure, the vision is always a prefiguration of the ultimate darkness of death. It figures prominently in Storm's prose as the local lore of a "Vorspuk" or "Vorgesicht," a kind of premonition implying a warning of some impending peril or catastrophe. It is important to note that the motif of the visionary is at once expansive and confining in character. While, on the one hand, it tends to function very much like the supernatural in his poetry, namely to perpetuate the moment, to expand, and transcend, the limits of time and space—akin to the role of the miracle in Romantic literature —it represents a limiting factor in the individual's life, on the other. As the common heritage of the people of Schleswig-Holstein, fear and superstitious beliefs held sway over the individual, obscuring his vision. The ambiguous role played by the supernatural is, in part, due to Storm's open-mindedness concerning such phenomena, causing him to plead the incomplete researches and discoveries of science in the realm of nature beyond common-sense perception.

In sum, clairvoyance as well as other folkloric elements in Storm's works are the result of a variety of causes. They are attributable to Storm's social environment, to the fact that his native Frisia, like Scotland, "was the home of clairvoyance" (Storm), to a personal predilection for the irrational, to the possibilities which the supernatural offered for a total cosmology as well as a defense against the drab materialism of his time, and, finally, to the political significance, in the 1840's, of preserving a cultural heritage.

II *Loneliness and the Demonic*

Loneliness and the demonic are further aspects of the horrible in Storm's work that deserve mention. In the collection of horror tales *Am Kamin*, the narrator analyzes the reason for man's profound loneliness: "Upon reflection, we must concede that each human being lives unto himself in terrible loneliness, a speck lost in infinite and incomprehensible space. We tend to forget that fact; but, at times, when we are confronted with the incomprehensible and the immense, we are suddenly gripped by an awareness thereof; and that, I should think, would be a little of what we have come to call horror." [5] But this sentimentalizing of man's loneliness—that is, envisioning man as a castaway in space, drifting through the void—is merely the extension of a motif found in many of Storm's works according to which men are terrified with loneliness when they are confronted by their own mortality. It is this existential loneliness in the face of death rather than the inexplicable, the weird, or the uncanny as such which evokes horror.

In many of Storm's novellas, the motif of the demonic occurs. On the one hand, it asserts itself in the lonely figures of the demonic women who, in their own right, represent the dark side of human nature. On the other hand, the occurrence of the demonic women in *Draussen im Heidedorf* and *Von jenseit des Meeres* represents the symbolic expression of rebellion against the established order on the part of the male characters who are attracted by these women. In the former novella, Hinrich Fehse rebels against his peasant background and morality, and in the latter Alfred disregards the racial prejudice of his social class by marrying Jenni who is half black. Moreover, the occurrence of these demonic characters signals the growing nationalism in Germany above which Storm was unable to rise. Hence, all of his demonic women are fully or partly foreign, that is, non-German. Finally, whatever may be the meaning of the supernatural and of the antibourgeois rebellion in Storm's works of the 1870's, it must be said that these motifs do not reach beyond the level of the potential. None of them is ever brought to its positive resolution.

The female characters, then, mainly by their animal magic, represent the chief occurrence of the demonic in his works. They "drain their victims' souls" [6] very much in the manner exemplified by the "weisse Alp" in *Draussen im Heidedorf*. "Der weisse Alp" is a nightmare, presumably having originated in the steppes of the lower Danube region, which was old Slavic territory. The main phenomenon of the nightmare is a ghoulish creature which grows from a "thin white thread" into a vampire and attacks the hapless sleeper by night. "On the following morning, everything has disappeared; but the sleeper who opens his eyes has become an imbecile overnight; the white nightmare has drained his soul. He will never recover it; the monster has carried it off into the damp recesses of the heath amid the moors and bogs." [7] The Slavic origin of this superstition serves Storm to depict the foreign element which threatens to destroy or, at the very least, disrupt the family and the closely knit community of a village in his native heath. Margarete Glansky, the daughter of the village midwife in the "Heidedorf" story, and her Slovak husband, are possessed by primitive instincts and she appears in the story as a vampire, a nightmare, and even a werewolf. Her fate and that of anyone coming into contact with her are foredoomed. Being the primitive she is, she is incapable of love. When blind passion threatens the personality, such sexuality ceases to have any purpose, even the purpose of procreation. In Storm's dualistic concept of nature, according to which life is a perpetual cycle of procreation and death, nature causes such primitive instinct to be self-destructive.

As already mentioned, in the era of German nationalism, the topic of distrust and disruption caused by the foreign and strange recurred repeatedly in German literature, and Storm shared in that prejudice. Specifically, Storm attributed a demonic character to such instances of foreignness in his works. Sometimes these characters are of Slavic descent, sometimes French, or Gypsy, or Slovak, or simply foreign—fully or partly non-German.[8] It is the factor of miscegenation which proves disastrous. Storm's demonic women are, almost without exception, a mixture of indigenous and foreign blood. This fact is sometimes indicated by the juxtaposition of native and foreign names: Margarete Glansky (*Dlaussen im Heidedorf*), Lore Beauregard (*Auf der Universität*), Botilla Jansen (*Im Nachbarhause links*), Oligard Swendrofski (*Die Armesünderglocke*).

Heredity also plays a role in the demonic side of Jenni (*Von jenseit des Meeres*, 1865). The dark side of Jenni's hereditary makeup concerns her black mother. Jenni's home is the Caribbean island of St. Croix, and she and her people are described as noble savages corrupted by their white masters and by miscegenation; "and, according to Charles Sealsfield's travelogue *Pflanzerleben,* [or popular report on the social conditions in the Americas] they are the evil spirits of the European immigrants because of their alluring beauty." [9] As a half-breed, Jenni is saved from self-destruction by the awareness of her "sinful origin" and its attendant dangers. Her German father makes it possible for her to be brought up in Germany, abandoning her friends and relations on St. Croix. Subsequently, she breaks the vicious circle of her heritage by her marriage to a German. Her mother's people to whom she is tied by her blood instill in her feelings of abject horror: "Here in this country I myself belong to them; I am of their blood, link by link the chain extends to me." [10] In the case of Jenni, as well as that of the other demonic women, it is the exotic element that attracts the narrator's and reader's attention. The irrational element in their lives forms part of Storm's concept of tragedy. It represents the unresolved mysteries of human existence which, like the supernatural, is viewed as causing suffering and as pointing to a higher human potential. It is part of Storm's "transcendental materialism," to coin a term. Storm's concept of the tragic was purely mechanical, with man (or the hero) attempting to struggle in vain against the inadequacies and limitations of the order of things and of mankind; and, in the process, the hero's undoing is called "most tragic of all." This fatalism in the face of an arbitrary and meaningless world order is held in abeyance only by Storm's devout belief in a symbolic meaning of life, as it is tacitly implied in the phenomenon of the demonic itself. The demonic female characters, including Jenni, represent the very antithesis of their staid middle- and peasant-class environments. There are social as well as hereditary barriers which prevent humanity from developing untrammeled.

Beyond the social conflict portrayed in terms of the demonic, Storm's profound perturbance over the lack of a rational answer to human existence is reflected in the motif. At the same time, it reflects his fascination with the transcendental potential of man implied in the inexplicable and unexplored aspects of his life. Storm himself suffered from the unresolved mystery of separation in his marriage with Constanze and his passionate relationship with Dorothea Jensen. It is also suggested by his demonic characters' resigned acceptance of their fate. Loneliness, that is to say, a complete reduction of all human relationships to one's own resilience or inherent weakness, is an essential fact of the human condition for Storm.

III *The Fairy Tales*

This element of loneliness as the psychological source for the motif of the demonic is of equal importance for Storm's fairy tales. Besides being interested in collecting folklore and legends, Storm actually wrote five fairy tales, two at the time of his active interest in the genre and the three others in a rash of productivity during the years 1863–64. The titles of his fairy tales are: *Der Kleine Häwelmann* (1849), *Hinzelmeier* (1850), *Bulemanns Haus, Die Regentrude,* and *Der Spiegel des Cyprianus,* all written between 1863 and 1864. At first glance, at least, these tales would seem to belong to the Romantic and *Biedermeier* category of literary fairy tales (*Kunstmärchen*). There is, however, some reason to doubt the accuracy of this term in view of their content and form.

We shall omit from our discussion *Der Kleine Häwelmann,* a children's tale of little importance for the genre as well as for Storm's prose as a whole. The question as to how successful Storm was in this genre remains problematical. Perhaps of the four stories, only *Die Regentrude* qualifies as a genuine fairy tale, whereas the others are mere allegories.

Hinzelmeier. Eine nachdenkliche Geschichte (1857) (*Hinzelmeier; a problematic tale*) is the earliest of Storm's "fairy tales," and, as the subtitle suggests, it is problematic indeed. The earlier version of 1850 carried the title *Stein und Rose. Ein Märchen* (*Stone and Rose. A Fairy Tale*), preceded by these couplets:

> Ein wenig Scherz in die ernste Zeit,
> Ein Lautenklang in den verwirrten Streit,
> In das politische Versegebell
> Ein rundes Märchenritornell! [11]

(A bit of humor into these serious times, a sound of the lute into this confusing strife, and into the political barking of rhymes, a round of fairy tales!)

The two versions of the tale differ only in some details. The fifth chapter was rewritten to accommodate some of Storm's critics with whose views he obviously agreed. From its inception, however, the escapist tendency and its allegorical and, therefore, reflective character were obvious and led Storm eventually to admit that "*Hinzelmeier* was more like a fantastic and allegorical composition in which the poet does not relate his story with complete conviction but stands somewhat reflectively beside it." [12] This self-criticism must be taken seriously, because of Storm's strict views about the "immediacy" of a work of art. (The effect on the critics was equally ambivalent.) The story concerns young Hinzelmeier's quest for the philosopher's stone. Hinzelmeier belongs to the order of masters of the rose whose members possess the secret of eternal youth. As a *Rosenherr* he must secure the rose destined for him, and along with it its caretaker, the rose maiden. From the moment Hinzelmeier decides to acquire a skill, things start to go wrong. He decides that this skill must be some great, yet unheard-of art. After spending a year with a great wizard, a cross between Faust and a medieval magician, Hinzelmeier is sent on his way with a motto and a raven with green glasses, which the master had made from a black hair of his beard. Hinzelmeier now pursues his great goal, which is the quest for the philosopher's stone. Three times in the story the raven drops his glasses on Hinzelmeier's nose, thereby completely changing the scene before his eyes. Each time, in this way, the raven prevents Hinzelmeier from returning with his rose maiden to the rose garden and eternal youth. Every nine years the maiden is allowed to leave her place by the rose belonging to its master to go out in the world in order to find him and to be freed from bondage. Hinzelmeier ages rapidly while his parents, who are also bearers of the secret and whom other people by now consider his children, remain youthful. Twice Hinzelmeier is able to remove the green glasses from his eyes. At one point, he sees Kasperle, another master of the rose gone astray, and at another his rose maiden. Both times his moment of truth has no consequences. Kasperle, who claims to have found the philosopher's stone, is really sitting on a big, hardened cheese, and when Hinzelmeier finally sees his maiden, he is at the point of death. Thus, in the end, Hinzelmeier is unsuccessful with either quest, and the rose maiden catches the raven, hurls it into the air, and the bird disappears. Then she plants the red rose by Hinzelmeier's grave and returns to the rose garden and eternal captivity.

The allegorical meaning of this tale of a fruitless quest for eternal youth and wisdom seems clear enough. The humor or irony of its style is perhaps the index of its real meaning, which is to ridicule a quest which must lead away from ordinary reality: the names of Hinzelmeier and Kasperle are clearly allusions to a philistine and a clown. The quest chapters of the story are told with a sense of detachment on the part of the narrator, while the chapters dealing with the rose maiden are related with the naïve tone of the folk tale. These stylistic ambiguities are further corroborated by the lack of conformity to established criteria for a fairy tale, such as the following: "The internal structure of the fairy tale is designed to lead to a moral satisfaction: as soon as we enter the world of the fairy tale we destroy the world of reality which is felt to be immoral . . . in this sense the miracle is not miraculous at all but perfectly natural . . . tragic are the endless obstacles placed in the way of the hero, and justice is to receive a treasure or to marry a prince." [13] The many literary fairy tales of the Romantics and the *Biedermeier* poets which are at variance with this basic structure are hybrid forms reflecting various historical factors inimical to the total world view of the traditional folk tale. In the case of all Storm's fairy tales, excepting perhaps *Die Regentrude,* there is no such moral satisfaction or real tragedy as is engendered by the conflict between a world felt to be immoral and our naïve ethical demands for redress of any wrongs. Hinzelmeier is a fool eliciting feelings of pity. The structural element of the miracle, which Jolles considered a basic trait of the conventional fairy tale, does not resolve itself as a "perfectly natural" occurrence. It is, rather, deflected and destroyed by its exposure as basic unreality. This is evident not only from the humorous and ironic style of the story but also from the events themselves: the philosopher's stone turns out to be a round cheese, the devil is revealed as a fool, the raven's colored glasses are revealed as a perfectly ordinary phenomenon, and Hinzelmeier's quest as a mere allegorization of a foolish mortal's struggle against the ravishes of time and death. The only guilt which Hinzelmeier incurs is that of a certain passivity, a lack of realism required by his descendance. This heritage could perhaps be defined as tending the family "garden" in the early years, to marry and to live in harmony with oneself and others (the rose garden, the youth motif, and the rose maiden). Hinzelmeier does not heed his parents' warnings that if he chased after a useless art (the philosopher's stone), he would end up like the neighbor's Kasperle (clown) who lost his rose maiden (youth or strength to cope with life) in pursuit of a fruitless goal. This, then, moves the tale of *Hinzelmeier* in the vicinity of the *Biedermeier* concept of reality,[14] a concept that denies a symbolic or transcendental meaning to reality, while regretting it. The apparent affirmation of the genre through its frequent use by the *Biedermeier* poets and by Storm, then, actually represents its negation. This is true for the other so-called fairy tales by Storm as well.

This apparent incongruity between the form of the fairy tale and its realistic content is even less concealed in the tales written between 1863 and 1865. The element of the demonic and supernatural, which is employed here in the context of a fairy tale, is to suggest a meaning inherent in the harsh and inexorable laws of transiency and death.[15] In this sense, the dualism between reality and the loss of a total meaning to life, or life's myths, is most effectively overcome in these fairy tales, even more so than in Storm's lyrics and certainly in his novellas. There is no illusory concept of an empirical reality which must justify and explain individual existence. They represent a conscious allegorization of life which employs the supernatural as a possible alternative to confining and isolating reality. The fairy tales, then, serve an end, both negative and affirmative: to show the impossibility of a Romantic and naïve flight from reality and to experiment with a new although tentative answer to a more profound meaning to life, whose truth is not merely circumscribed by practical reality alone.

Storm was fully aware of all that. This becomes clear from his preface to the first edition of his fairy tales of 1865. Of course, he apologizes for his stories whose only reason for being should be sought in the reader's need to escape from unpleasant reality; but he really hopes to coax his audience into accepting a less prosaic view of life:

If I called these stories fairy tales, I must ask that this not be taken too seriously; the Cyprianus-mirror tale is probably closer to the more distinguished tone of the legend. "Bulemanns Haus" should be more accurately called a curious chronicle; but there is the element of the fantastic which they have in common and which must justify the chosen designation. . . . And so, this time, I shall invite, besides the old, also the young to be daring and to take with me "the journey to the old Romantic land." The progress will be gentle, to be sure, but in the end, nevertheless, it will take us nicely beyond the workaday world. . . ." [16]

In the preface to the second edition of 1873, Storm regrets the scant success of the first and attributes it to his prosaic age which no longer believes in fairy tales. Even his explanation that these fairy tales are only such by virtue of their designation seems to have been of no avail, and thus he once more assures the reader that "the trip will not take too long and will not soar too steeply to cause dizziness in the practically-minded heads of our modern times." [17]

Bulemanns Haus relates the story of an old man whose curse is that he cannot die. Bulemann's crime was his greed and the death of a child caused by him. The grave of the child and the "grave" of his deteriorating house serve as symbols of crime and punishment. The threatening demons in Bulemann's life do not occupy an imagined and distant hell, but live within and near him. The two cats in his house grow bigger and bigger until they become Bulemann's tormentors and jailors. "Only God's mercy can release him" is the concluding line of this uncanny tale, dwelling upon the demonic side of the human soul.

Cyprianus' Mirror again pursues the theme of crime and punishment. The mirror serves as a reflection of man's hopes, desires, and passions. Cyprianus, the master, warns that the mirror must never be the witness of a foul deed and that only the culprit's blood could atone for it and could restore the healing power of the looking glass. The mirror is a magical and demonic, as well as natural, force. The demonic aspect of the primitive concept of crime and retribution becomes an ethical and psychological one. Love casts out the shadow of a past crime (murder) in the manor of the countess and banishes the curse attached to the mirror which had once reflected the crime.

It is only in the *Regentrude* tale that Storm succeeds in completely blending the real and the fantastic, which makes this a "fairy tale" that does not expose the supernatural as unreal and the real as too confining. Rather, it shows the magic forces of life to be an extension of the real world. The realms of the rain maiden and of the village are complementary. Nature and man need the maiden, just as she needs them. This is symbolized by her awakening from the sleep into which she had been forced by evil demons. The dying and the revival of nature are described at the beginning and the end of the story, respectively. The major part of the story is filled with the search for the rain maiden, her discovery and awakening after many trials, and the trickery used by Andrees and Maren, the young lovers from the village, in obtaining the magic word for Regentrude's release. This story, then, fulfills most of the structural demands for the traditional folk tale. Yet, more important, it is—with one exception—the only time Storm was able to resolve his lifelong personal and artistic struggle with the problem of the spiritual and material aspects of reality by affirming both. Only his last novella, *Der Schimmelreiter*, fulfills this same ideal and represents the culmination of his formal and thematic efforts in achieving a perfect fusion of myth and reality, of chronicle and drama, a novella that does not need the nostalgic trapping of a fairy tale in the search for life's hidden meaning, nor the conclusion that a cold and pragmatic world has destroyed that meaning and its outward form, the fairy tale.

CHAPTER 4

The Novellas

OVER the years much has been said about Storm's overriding concern with transiency and death in his novellistic oeuvre. While in search of a transcendental meaning to life, it has been said, he was forced to acknowledge the limits of the human condition which is circumscribed by society, heredity, and death. All that is not to be denied. Yet, it would appear that, from the very beginning, Storm's instinctive world view was one that felt human existence to be tragic—not so much by virtue of his explicit definition of tragedy as by implication through style and form, motif and narrative perspective, which define the narrator's attitude toward his fictitious world. From Storm's lyrical canon of the immediate, untrammeled experience to the emotional atmosphere of his novellas, there is a consistent struggle with the tragic meaning of life as confronted with material reality, suggesting a merely mechanistic function for individual existence. In order to establish the scope and meaning of Storm's prose, it is not only necessary to discuss its major themes but also its structural components, for they are to bear out the contention of a tragic view of life and an attempted solution culminating in a new myth of tragic man.

From a merely typological point of view, Storm's novellas show a fixed number of recurring forms and themes. Of a total of fifty-six novellas, fairy tales, and vignettes, forty-three can properly be called novellas. Twenty-six of these, or more than half, are frame tales. If we count the other prose pieces as well, approximately one half of his prose works are told by a narrator-character, either as the main character of the story or as a minor character. This narrator tells his story and plays his role most frequently in the first person and occasionally in the third person. The other half of the novellas are related by the author-narrator, again, either in the first or in the third person. Throughout his oeuvre, Storm never appears undisguised as the author, addressing his readers in a free

and sovereign manner using humor, irony, or wit. In fact, it can
be said that Storm was intent upon concealing his personal involvement as the author of his fiction.[1] The obvious question arising from these facts relates to the possible reasons for this reticence
and for this preference for the frame-tale novella and the manuscript fiction of his later novellas.

The novella and the frame tale are, of course, conventions of
the nineteenth century, in a sense, in which Storm simply shared.
These conventions, of course, assumed special Stormian forms, reflecting their author's creative transformation; whereas the reasons
for the particular preferences of form in Storm's novellas are as
personal as they are complex.

We have already hinted at Storm's struggle with a metaphysic
of life in an age that profoundly discouraged such a view. We
must examine whether, like Hölderlin, Storm was reluctant to be
"a poet in paltry times" or whether he was too sensitive to endure
the peal of scornful laughter by the contemporary critics of his romanticism and escapism, as one might be led to believe from his
prefatory remarks to the second edition of his "Märchen." There
are, moreover, questions to be answered regarding the obvious
conventionality of his images and metaphors in his lyric and his
prose, as well as the rich evidence for his escapist attitudes of
sentimental resignation and political inactivity and his, at times,
purely esthetic view of life. There is evidence, on the other hand,
that Storm could rise to a point of view similar to that of Friedrich
Nietzsche, the great moralist, visionary, and idealistic gadfly of
the pedestrian age of Bismarck. The contradictions, finally, are
most likely and plausibly resolved by the assumption of a demon-
strable vulnerability, of a weakness borne of self-doubt and profound insecurity, and of an intellectual mediocrity from which
Storm was able to free himself only in rare but exalted moments.
To say this is not to deny his artistry or his quality as a poet. It is
to say, rather, that Storm had his limitations which, incidentally,
were largely known to him and which become evident upon a
close examination of his works.

These questions and the tentative answers to them given above
have been raised and resolved before in various ways. Storm's
preference for the frame-tale novella has been explained as reflecting an inner need to create a situation of audience and story-
teller.[2] Another critic interprets the frame as amplifying the

atmospheric element of the relation between the "Then" of the interior tale and the "Now" of the frame.[3] Finally, the frame has been interpreted to symbolize a constant struggle by Storm with himself and his sources by serving to mask or reveal a personal connection with his story.[4] The distance created by the frame as well as the "manuscript fiction" and the effort to create the impression on the reader that he is a participant or, at least, intimate observer of the action represent another conclusion about Storm's prose work.[5] Of all the extant typological studies, the leading and most painstaking is that by Clifford Bernd [6] who concludes that Storm's novellas reveal the narrator's constant struggle between reminiscence and transiency, a fact which accounts for the form of his novellas. All of these scholars have emphasized Storm's strong emotional attachment to homeland and family, to his wife and children and his friends. They have stressed Storm's separation of the bourgeois world of social class and profession from the artistic realm, and, last but not least, they have pointed to the overriding importance of Storm's personal fear of death and transiency and its manifestation as literary motifs in his works. Thus, the theme of transiency and death has been considered to account for the structure of Storm's frame and manuscript novellas.[7]

In the following analysis of eight of Storm's novellas,[8] particular attention will be given to the importance of the tragic aspects of his fiction. Unlike previous studies, ours attempts to show that Storm's work represents a fairly consistent struggle with a pessimistic philosophy which is eventually transformed into a new myth of tragic man in *Der Schimmelreiter*. The typological criteria used in selecting the novellas tend to corroborate the fact that Storm's tragic view of life largely determined the structure of these novellas.

I *Immensee*

Immensee (1849) was the one work which brought Storm to the attention of a wider circle of readers. To this day, it is his most widely read and translated novella, its first translation into English by Helene Clark dating back to the poet's own lifetime. The story represents Storm's first frame-tale novella. What had gone before were sketches and vignettes. The first version of *Immensee* appeared in 1849. Given its theme of unrequited love, it is an astounding document of Storm's determination to place an inward

experience before the issues of the day culminating in the turbu-
lence of the year 1848. Because of the scathing critique of the novella by Tycho Mommsen, Storm revised it and published it in
1851 in its present form.[9] The story concerns the reminiscences of
its main character who appears in the opening part of the frame
as an old man. As Reinhard, the old man and poet, looks at an old
picture of a young woman, he mutters "Elisabeth," and "as he had
spoken the word, time was changed—he had returned to his
youth." [10] Thus we are taken into Reinhard's past, and his story is
recalled for us piece by piece in separate little scenes, each with
its own chapter heading. Reinhard and Elisabeth already loved
one another as children. Because of Reinhard's impractical nature
and his failure to be an adequate provider, Elisabeth marries another man. She does not love that man, but she obeys her mother's
wish. Reinhard's rival is Erich, a childhood friend. Two years
pass. Reinhard is invited to visit Erich at his estate, "Immensee,"
and he is received without guile. One evening, Reinhard and his
friends are sitting together singing folk songs. A song which Reinhard has recorded reveals that Elisabeth still loves him, indeed,
more fervently than ever, because they cannot love each other
openly. The song's opening lines state the reason for Elisabeth's
marriage to Erich: "My mother willed it, / The other one I had to
wed. / What had been mine before, / My heart was to forget; /
That it did not want to do." [11] And then, "While Reinhard was
reading, he felt an imperceptible trembling of the paper; when he
had finished, Elisabeth quietly pushed back her chair and went
down to the garden in silence." [12] Erich and Elisabeth, the unhappy couple, must resign themselves to their fate just as Reinhard and Elisabeth. When Reinhard takes his leave, Elisabeth
says to him, "You won't come back, I know it, don't lie to me; you
will never come back." "Never," he says. Elisabeth's hand drops,
and her attitude is one of utter resignation. Reinhard quickly
leaves, "and more and more the quiet place disappeared behind
him, and before him appeared the big wide world." The next
chapter takes the reader back to the situation of the opening
frame. The lonely old man returns to his books, and "he pored
over his studies at which he had once tested the strength of his
youth."

From this simple plot, Storm develops his art of allusion and
symbolism. The atmosphere of quiet renunciation and of the re-

lentless passage of time permeates this story, which frequently borders on the sentimental and saccharine. From the very beginning, it is evident how relatively formless and fluid the characters are. Neither their activities nor their appearances are examined and developed. The conventionality of Storm's language and imagery, furthermore, is obvious. Nevertheless, the blandness of its characters and its style make this novella typically Stormian. Before embarking on the scrutiny of the style and structure of the story, the reason for this blandness and ordinariness ought to be given. It is simply Storm's technique to involve the reader emotionally in as profound a way as he himself was moved by the fable of his novella, namely by the tragic aspects of human existence which is circumscribed by ultimate personal isolation and death. Its profoundly moving theme of reminiscence and transiency is what had to be imparted to the reader as an immediate experience, as untrammeled as its author had experienced it. This Storm achieved by the subtle and sparing use of a small number of symbolic gestures and actions.

The most striking of the symbolic gestures in *Immensee,* as well as in other novellas from Storm's early and middle periods, are those of the outstretched arms and expressive eyes. They both have a strong emotional content. When Reinhard takes his leave from Elisabeth, his frustration and her utter despair are expressed solely by means of gestures: "She stood motionless and looked at him with lifeless eyes. He took a step forward and moved his outstretched arms toward her. Then he forced himself to turn away and walked through the door." [13] Another symbolic expression typical for Stormian characters is conveyed by the hands of a person. As far as *Immensee* is concerned, these emotionally expressive hands are Heine reminiscences, a fact which, among others, proves Storm's dependence on literary models at the time.[14] Thus, for example, Elisabeth's hands, at one point, reveal her inner state of sorrow:

And this pale hand revealed what her face had concealed from him. He saw that delicate line of hidden sorrow on it which frequently finds its expression through the beautiful hands of women which come to rest by night on a wounded heart.—When Elisabeth felt his eyes resting on her hand, she let it drop slowly over the side [of the boat] into the water.[15]

This emphasis on the profound emotions of his characters was a point of which Storm was acutely aware. It implied a basic attitude toward life on his part. It had, as its basis, a strong conviction of the essentially tragic nature of human existence. It limited the author, however, to a largely "atmospheric" style which worked at the expense of vividness and lucidity of character portrayal. A rather telling episode, in this connection, is the brief passage in a letter to his wife, where he mentions that he has just reread his prose sketch *Im Sonnenschein* (1854): ". . . and I, the author, was once again completely overwhelmed by this poesy of evanescence." [16] This problem of projecting his own convictions and experiences upon the material of his fiction was a constant source of vexation for him. His sensitivity to criticism in this regard caused him frequently to make changes for the sake of an immediate impact on the reader. In a letter to his friend, the Hebbel biographer Emil Kuh, Storm claimed to have overcome his difficulty of projecting his emotional attitude on the characters of his novella *Draussen im Heidedorf* (1872): "[This proves] that I am able to write a novella without the lingering atmosphere of a certain mood (that is to say, of a mood which is not, from the beginning, brought to the story by its author [according to Heyse and Kurz the lyrical novella], but which develops naturally from the facts themselves in the process of reading)." [17] In connection with the Gypsy girl episode in *Immensee*, Storm commented on the basically tragic experience of life which he was moved to convey. When Reinhard visits the Ratskeller on Christmas Eve, the beautiful Gypsy, amid the banter and laughter, sings a song with the *carpe diem* motif of transiency and death that reminds him of his love for Elisabeth and which prefigures their unhappy fate. Storm wrote:

It is a fact of human nature, in which the feeling of finiteness struggles with that of infinity, that we are overcome by the most powerful pain of the inevitable end precisely at the moment and peak of fullest pleasure. . . . The "Song of the Girl with the Harp" [the Gypsy girl], however, expresses the anguish and sorrow of a painful existence as it can be produced only by passionate love.[18]

The profound pessimism and tragic view of life which speak from these lines also speak from the symbols employed in *Im-*

mensee, all of which serve in the last analysis, to "let the facts speak for themselves" and to move the reader profoundly. For example, in the early stories *Immensee, Angelika,* and *Viola tricolor,* lakes are the scenes of passive renunciation. They symbolize the precariousness of human relationships. Reinhard's and Elisabeth's boat ride on the "Immen" lake reveals Elisabeth's quiet suffering and the futility of their love. Later, when Reinhard swims out to fetch a water lily for Elisabeth, he is unable to reach it, because he gets entangled in the weeds which threaten to pull him down. The water is a symbol of man's tragic limitations—in this instance, man's limitation by natural forces. "He suddenly had a feeling of anxiety in the strange element," it is said of Reinhard as he swims to reach the lily.[19]

In *Immensee* birds[20] echo various motifs which, by their indirection, serve to heighten the emotional content of these motifs. When, for instance, the linnet which Reinhard had given to Elisabeth dies, their relationship changes also, because the linnet is replaced by a canary, a gift from Erich, Reinhard's practically minded and successful rival. As an undomesticated or wild bird, the linnet is symbolic of Reinhard, whereas the canary is more in keeping with the "domesticated" or civilized Erich. The canary sits in a gilded cage and pecks at Elisabeth's finger, symbolizing her gilded captivity. Elisabeth cannot understand why Reinhard does not like the bird. Finally, it is a bird which signals the conclusion of the novella. After the boat ride, the hopelessness of the couple's situation is clear. The birds stop singing. When Reinhard leaves Immensee at dawn, the first lark streaks jubilantly skyward, much like Shakespeare's in *Romeo and Juliet,* to signal their parting.

Another instance of a striking symbolism in *Immensee* bears mentioning. In their youth, upon the occasion of a picnic in the woods, the women stay behind to prepare the repast while the men go out to bring what they can find. While Erich returns with wild strawberries, Reinhard comes back with a poem for Elisabeth, again stressing his impractical and undomesticated or independent nature. The fact that Reinhard, the main character of the story and the frame, is a poet links him directly with the invisible third-person narrator, namely the author-poet. This is one of many examples where Storm, in spite of all his efforts to assume an objective stance toward his material, reveals himself as an al-

most immediate participant in the events of the story. This participation is not so much one suggested by actual parallels to his own
life as one indicated by the intense inwardness of the characters
with whom he sympathizes. This structural property of *Immensee*
corroborates what has been pointed out earlier in connection with
Storm's propensity for "atmospheric" values. This veritable inun-
dation of a carefully constructed bastion represented by the
framed novella and the objective third-person style points to an
essential dilemma for Storm: how to integrate private experience
with isolated, fragmented reality to make a meaningful whole giving the illusion of objective validity. In order to heal this breach
or, rather, in order to transcend it, Storm finally succeeded, in *Der
Schimmelreiter,* in creating a mythical figure whose material reality no longer depended on the creation of an illusory objective
frame of reference. Reinhard's ambiguous role as a dedicated artist and an inadequate provider and Storm's own doubts as to his
role in society may be inferred. By and large, he considered it
essential that the poet and writer be well integrated into society
by having a profession outside his calling. Yet, here and there we
find examples for a feeling of isolation from society as a whole
which is reminiscent of the conflict between art and life as portrayed in Thomas Mann's *Tonio Kröger* or in Eduard Mörike's
Maler Nolten (*Nolten the Painter*) before him.

Storm's poem "Hyacinths" (1852) expresses the suffering of the
poet who must view the object of his love and desire from the
outside. "I would like to sleep, but you have to dance." Just like his
author, Reinhard, the poet and lover, is condemned to observe and
suffer and never to participate in life's happiness. Storm once confessed that he could only "ascend to the lofty realm of dreams
without a care if Constanze's hand held me close to my homeland
soil." [21] This statement reveals that he perceived a rift between art
and reality which he could only overcome in the knowledge of
being securely anchored to homeland and family. These, perhaps,
represented the only truly meaningful quantities in his life. Indeed, after Constanze's death, Storm was convinced that he could
no longer write or command his muse, and he published his collected works in 1868 as a final gesture. Storm's insecurity concerning his attitude as an author toward his fiction has been docu-
mented by one very telling example. He always concealed his

authorship except once in *Der Amtschirurgus* (1870). Here, he freely converses with his muse, saying:

Through the open window drifts the aroma of primroses from the garden and, outside, under the budding syringa tree suddenly stands my muse, whom I had not seen for so long. She throws back her beautiful, eternally youthful head and looks at me; the springtime sun reflects her golden hair. Shall I once more walk along your dreamlike paths? But what if you lead me to the heights and your foot leaves the firm earth and treads upon the rosy clouds? To be sure, my soul still has its wings; but many of the lifting feathers have been broken already, and I sense the pull of the earth more strongly than usual. But who could resist these eyes? Let us go then! Brush aside with your godly hand the graying hair from my temples, and then tell me: how did it happen? [22]

These opening lines reveal Storm to be out of character, using the clichés of classical convention without a correspondingly lofty subject to justify it.

The acceptance by society, the security afforded by the familiarity of home and family were essential to Storm for his well-being and his productivity. It is, therefore, not surprising that he felt he had to conceal his strong emotional involvement with his fiction by interposing a narrator merely resembling the author or by employing a first-person narrator who plays a role in the narrative as well. This limitation of his art should ultimately be viewed as a positive feature insofar as he was unable to assume the ironic attitude of the novelist toward his fictitious world. The frame of *Immensee* is meant to mask Storm's involvement—his love for Bertha von Buchan, who is said to have provided the model for Elisabeth[23]—in addition to the already mentioned parallel between Reinhard and Storm. The illusion of reality is created by the frame which justifies the telling of the story by arousing the reader's curiosity. In most of his novellas, Storm is forever recalling something, in order to rescue from oblivion a part of reality that was important to him and to focus attention on that reality, elevating it, as it were, to a superior status with great significance for the present. For him, the tragic meaning of life lies in the time factor (its relentless passage) and in the values of ethos and humanism, depicted in his stories, which his own time had begun to erode and to destroy. The "hermetic" form of the novella—its "objective" character based on the assumption of an orderly universe or frame of reference universally valid and entirely controllable by the poet—was Storm's vehicle for the expression of his struggle with a meaning for life. By this logic, the novella was the ideal means to preserve the appearance of orderliness (just as the social institutions of nineteenth-century Germany belied their manifestly chaotic character, i.e., the spiritual vacuum in which people lived), and, hence, Storm considered the novella capable of expressing even the noblest subjects, such as had previously been the exclusive province of the drama; and so he once called the novella "the sister of the drama." [24]

Storm's intention to move the reader profoundly—"one thing I would regret very much: if my fiction were merely pathetic. It ought to be tragic" [25]—stems from a desire to change or, at least, influence his own age in seeking out deeper human and ethical values. Moreover, the years after 1870, years of crass materialism and colonial expansion, required the total mobilization of the poet's defenses; hence, Storm wished to employ his art, as he once told his reading public, "in order to afford entry, for a short while, into an ideal world, into a world individually limited, away from an enormous vastness, from a stern and wearisome reality. In this ideal world, struggle and guilt exist just as they do in the real world, but they are contained within the peacefulness of art and redeemed by it." [26] This form of escapism should not be regarded exclusively as a nonanswer to a serious dilemma, but also as Storm's way of functioning in the most meaningful way possible, namely as a humanist and moralist, rather than as a literary model for social change and justice.

After two decades, in 1875, Storm's literary craft reached its first climax with the writing of *Aquis submersus*.

II *Aquis submersus*

This story belongs to the so-called historical or chronicle novellas by Storm. These novellas are all located in the fairly distant past, and their core or legend is "rescued" from oblivion by the author-narrator. [27] The frame of *Aquis submersus* opens with the description of the circumstances which lead to the discovery of the manuscript containing the actual story. The locale for the second part of the story is the same as the place where the narrator comes upon the mysterious painting which so absorbs his interest. The events in the opening frame concern the personal account of the narrator. In a village near Husum,[28] two boys, the narrator and his friend, come upon two portraits in the village church on which the year 1666 is inscribed. One represents a man with the collar of a priest and the other a boy, about five-years-old, who is holding a white water-lily. The caption under this painting of the child reads "C.P.A.S.," which, according to legend and to the speculation of the narrator means "culpa patris aquis submersus" ("drowned through the fault of the father").[29] After many years have passed, we see the narrator as a young man on a walk through his hometown, not far from the village housing the paintings. In search of a room for a fellow student, his attention is attracted by a Low German epigraph above a doorway: "Just as smoke and dust vanish, so does man." Curious, he enters the house to inquire about a room. Inside, he discovers an old oil painting which looks strangely familiar, and representing a man in seventeenth-century dress, holding in his arms a boy whose small dangling hand is holding a water-lily. He knows that it is the same man and child whose portraits he had seen, years ago, in that village church. Upon questioning, the owner replies that the painting was passed down from his forebears, one of whom was the painter of the picture. In the course of their conversation, the man produces an old manuscript by that painter, and the narrator —"completely oblivious to all else"—proceeds to read the painter's personal account of his life:

In the year 1661, the young painter, whose name is Johannes, returns from a five-year apprenticeship in Amsterdam to his home in the "Holstenland." His home is the estate of Squire Gerhardus, a friend of his dead father. Johannes and Gerhardus' children, Master Wulf and Katharina, have grown up together. Johannes' sensitivity and honest character and Katharina's loveliness and innocence establish a close bond between them. Wulf and his friend Kurt von der Risch, however, have always behaved with arrogance and hostility toward Johannes who, by birth, was a commoner and therefore not their social equal. Now Johannes enters the house and learns of Squire Gerhardus' death. Wulf is now the squire. He has decided that his sister is to marry the young Baron von der Risch, whom Katharina detests. Since it is customary to paint the picture of a young lady of noble birth who is about to marry, Wulf orders Johannes to paint Katharina's picture. During that time, Johannes and Katharina confess their love for one another. These sessions are hours of great happiness for them, with no one present. The only jarring note is provided by the portrait of one of Katharina's ancestors who seems to be looking down on the young couple disapprovingly. Johannes expresses his aversion to the cold and staring eyes of this ancestral lady. Katharina has always had a similar feeling about the picture and remarks that the lady is said to have put a curse on her only child, "and on the next morning the child was drowned." The woman had cursed her child because she did not love the man whom she was forced to marry. The lady was in love with a man who was socially beneath her. The eyes of this ancestor remind Johannes and Katharina of Wulf's cold stare. The parallel to their own situation is clear to them. To escape from her intolerable situation and from a marriage she does not want, Katharina plans to leave her home in secret to live with an aunt in another town. Johannes promises to help. Returning from a secret errand in Katharina's behalf, Johannes, Wulf, and Kurt von der Risch accidentally meet in a roadside tavern. Wulf and Kurt are drunk, and, after an argument, Wulf unleashes his bloodhounds upon Johannes, who is chased the whole way to the estate and is forced to scale the wall of the manor. Katharina, awakened by the noise, opens her window, and Johannes stays in the arms of his beloved until daybreak. He had been seen entering Katharina's room, however, and to head off scandal and disgrace, he immediately asks Wulf for his sister's hand in marriage. Wulf's answer is a shot from his pistol, and Johannes, badly wounded, flees and spends many weeks in the care of a friend. He decides to return to Amsterdam but becomes too homesick to stay there. On his second return to the estate, he learns that Kurt von der Risch has married someone else, but he cannot get the one answer which he had hoped for. Katharina has vanished without a trace. At this point, the first part of the manuscript ends.

Johannes' report resumes with the year 1666. In a town on the North Sea, Johannes has been commissioned to paint several portraits and is called to a nearby village (the village mentioned in the opening frame) to paint a picture of the parson for the church. The parson is holding a young boy called Johannes by the hand. The boy's eyes inadvertently remind the painter of Katharina. One day he and Katharina unexpectedly meet in the garden of the rectory. She had been forced by her brother to marry the parson when it became clear that she was with child—Johannes' child. At this moment, they hear their child singing and playing nearby. Katharina wants to make sure that the child is safe where he is, but Johannes holds her back, and while they embrace, the child drowns in the pond of the garden. On the following day, at the request of Katharina's husband, Johannes paints the dead child and places a water-lily in his hand. Under the painting he sets the letters C.P.A.S. After telling his readers of Wulf's violent death from the bite of a rabid dog and of the passing of Squire Gerhardus' estate into the hands of strangers, Johannes concludes his story.

In the closing frame, the author-narrator appears once more to remark that Johannes' name cannot be found in any dictionary of biography. Even in his native region it is forgotten—"aquis submersus."

In this novella, Storm for the first time develops, around the motifs of love, passion, heredity, evanescence, and death (to name the most important ones), his concept of tragic guilt. The two factors which prove the undoing of the main characters, are the strictures of social convention, custom, and heredity, which function deterministically. Its mechanistic character does not entirely resolve the question of guilt for the first part of the narrative, however. The assumption of personal guilt in the boy's death does not answer the question satisfactorily for the second part either. Storm's own comment on his story stresses his deterministic view of tragic guilt:

In *Aquis submersus* one would be quite mistaken to seek the tragic guilt in the passionate union of the couple, disregarding any existing moral code proscribing such behavior. This, according to a comment by the author himself, was as far from his mind as from Shakespeare's when he wrote *Romeo and Juliet*. The "guilt," if one wants to retain this term, lies with the other side; here with the merciless family hatred, and there with the hubris of a fraction of society which considers itself superior—without any basis in personal merit—merely by insisting on some exceptional position usurped, at one time, by its ancestors. With this inherited power whatever is human, beautiful, and justified is destroyed; and it cannot be overlooked that it is precisely this hostile force which almost blindly drives the couple into each other's arms.[30]

Upon another occasion, three years earlier, and in answer to some criticism, Storm insisted that the Aristotelian definition of tragic guilt as some form of personal guilt, tragic flaw, or immoral behavior was too narrow. He stressed that what struck him as the most tragic thing of all was the undoing of the tragic hero by forces beyond his control which set natural limits to mankind. He called this "the inadequacy of the whole" of which the hero is a part and against which he struggles in vain. Storm remarked in this connection that *Aquis submersus* belonged in this discussion because he had not thought of any guilt on the part of the couple.[31] This relativistic determinism is not surprising in an age devoid of a unifying metaphysical concept. It is, however, not an extension of the Aristotelian concept of tragedy (Storm concludes this particular entry in his diary by speculating whether or not a distinction should be made between epic and dramatic tragedy) but a concept which is actually nihilistic. The death of the hero by accidental forces is a meaningless death. Storm's mechanistic concept of tragic guilt is closer to modern pathos than to Aristotelian catharsis.

In the predetermined scheme of things, Katharina's and Johannes' fate creates neither pity nor fear in the reader, unless one views their sacrifice in terms of a historical struggle which eventually resulted in the subjugation and conquest of the nobility by the middle class.[32] Quite in keeping with the bent of his own time, Storm placed the greatest emphasis on the factor of heredity in both the biological and sociological sense. Johannes' and Katharina's tragedy is due to Johannes' lower station in life and to the inherited evil traits in Wulf, the successor to Gerhardus, Johannes' father's benefactor and friend.

There are two leitmotifs which dominate the narrative and which stress the importance of the determinant of heredity: the eyes of the ancestor, of Wulf, of the dead boy, and of the two lovers, and the motif of drowning, which relates to the first motif as if by cause and effect. Thus, in the final scene, the death of young Johannes and the unhappy lives of his parents are attributable to this chain of events which was begun by an inexplicably cruel quirk of nature in the person of Wulf's female ancestor whose sins are visited on him and everyone connected with him by the bond of blood and circumstances. This distant ancestor once caused her child to drown, and her guilt and fate repeat themselves several generations hence.

In this narrative the eyes play a similar role to that of the hands in *Immensee*. Their expressiveness is an index of the character's emotional state. This motif, among others, serves to amplify the tragic character of the story or the intention of the author to create a tragic affect. The ancestor's eyes create a feeling of intense discomfort and even fear in Johannes: "As I was painting, my gaze fell upon that old portrait of a woman which hung at my side and which kept its piercing grey eyes trained on me from under her white veil. I was shivering, I nearly moved my chair." Katharina asks, "You almost turned pale, what has come over you, Johannes?" [33] Later, her eyes tell Johannes that she loves him: "And as she raised the lashes from the brown stars of her eyes, it could no longer be denied; fervently and openly their light went straight to my heart. 'Katharina!' " [34] When Johannes paints his dead child, it is again the eyes that tell of his thoughts: "I bent over his body in the illusion that I might once more look into the eyes of my child; but when the cold stars of his eyes lay before me, I was overcome by horror; I felt as if I were seeing the eyes of that ancestor of the family, as if they wished to speak from the face of the dead child even here: 'My curse has caught up with you both, after all!' " [35]

The motif of drowning is brought to its final climax by the priest who says: "Both parents let the child drown . . . the woman is lying by the dead body and is crying to God of her sins. Do not go to them for the sake of her poor soul!" [36] Johannes, however, believes that it was his fault and when he has finished his picture, with red paint he sets the letters C.P.A.S. under the portrait: "These were to signify *culpa patris aquis submersus*, 'vanished in the flood through the father's fault.' " [37] Ultimately, the meaning of the motif is extended to signal the transitoriness of all life, and the narrator's story concludes: "My old wound burned inside me; and, strangely, what I had never noticed before, I suddenly became aware that I could hear the surf breaking upon the distant shore. Not a soul crossed my path, I could not hear a single bird; but from the dark roar of the sea sounded the constant breaking of the waves as from a sinister lullaby: aquis submersus —aquis submersus!" [38]

To return once more to the question of tragic guilt, it would appear, then, that Storm sheds light on it from various perspectives. The possibility is conceded that not only the circumstances of heredity and social custom are at fault, but also Johannes and Katharina, whose passion blinds them momentarily to their duty to the unattended child. If this is to mean that passion is a flaw in the weave which can be the cause of tragic guilt, it could just as easily be seen in the context of a tragic existence shared by all men in terms of Storm's definition.

As we have noted earlier, in both parts the question of guilt cannot be answered satisfactorily on the basis of any single concept. What may be nearer the truth concerning *Aquis submersus* is its theme of transitoriness culminating in the idea expressed in the epigraph above the doorway of the house where the manuscript is found: "Just as smoke and dust vanish, so does man." The story of Johannes, Katharina, and Wulf—regardless of the final answer to the problem of guilt—is not nearly as tragic in the end as the fact of ultimate oblivion for all things on earth. Therefore, to the extent to which the guilt of the three main characters could be regarded as personal, the novella is tragic. Its overriding theme of evanescence (signaled by the leitmotif of drowning and the motif of the epigraph) and its moral and ethical determinism, however, lend it a pathetic character, indeed, even a sentimental one, if we consider the conclusion of the second part of Johannes' narrative quoted above.

These points are corroborated by the structure and composition of the novella. As has already been pointed out, the story is told by two persons, the author-narrator and the character-narrator. Both tell of their experiences in the first-person singular. The reason for this becomes readily apparent if we take our cues from the text itself and from what Storm himself said about the tragic emotion he wished to create in his readers. At the very beginning of the story, the author-narrator wishes us to see what only he can see, and he makes that intention very clear:

Most people would probably gaze westward, in order to marvel at the light green of the marshes and the silvery sea beyond, upon which floats the shadow of the elongated shape of the island; *my* eyes inadvertently turn northward where, barely a mile away, the grey, pointed church steeple rises from the coastal plain which is situated on higher ground but desolate; because there lies one of the places of my youth.[39]

The narrator then leaves the present in order to recall the events of his youth, brought to the surface by the haunting memories which the place evokes in him. We are taken to the church whose steeple is visible from a distance and which houses the oil paintings. After this and a visible caesura in the text, the narrator resumes his preliminary remarks (many years have passed) and takes us to the place where the manuscript is kept, where he proceeds to read it.

The manuscript itself consists of two parts. At the end of the first part, the narrator looks at the wall opposite him with the paintings of the boy and his father and then sets out to read the second part which opens with the epigraph that appears in the frame of the story, or in the narrative present, thereby establishing a close link between the past and the present. Indeed, all of the references to places in the present and the past of the manuscript story serve to emphasize the close connection Storm wishes to establish between the reader and his material. The first-person perspective of both narratives (the frame and the interior story) stresses the "authenticity" of the tale because the events are gradually recalled and rescued from a distant past. First, they are recalled from the author-narrator's own time, then from a point in his past (his youth), and finally from the time of the events described in the manuscript. The manuscript is in two parts because the writer, Johannes—just like the narrator of the frame, the author—retrieves the events of his life in stages, as if he were struggling against time and a fading memory which can only retain what seems important to it.[40]

This somewhat complicated structure of the novella is the result of Storm's need to gain the reader's confidence in the credibility of his story. Therefore, if the author's experience is to be taken by his reading public as having general validity, the writer must do what he actually does, namely make the reader forget that the recollected events represent private experiences in which he is not a participant. Hence he contrives to make his audience a witness to the manuscript story by having it receive the report first hand, from the mouth of the main character himself, as it were. Again, Storm is intent upon establishing a connection between himself and the reader and between the chronological parts of the novella itself. The main locations of the story are identical with the places referred to in the frame, a fact which gives us the clue to the ultimate meaning of the work: namely the transitoriness of all things as the reason for tragic human existence. For, obviously, if the poet had not noticed and retold the story, it would most certainly have been forgotten, because neither the village priest nor the house owner remembers or cares enough about the pictures and the manuscript and because, eventually, even the places themselves will begin to crumble and disappear. Moreover, the devices of the manuscript and the frame tale lend authenticity to the tragic events, thereby stressing their universal character and validity.

This illusion of reality—or the basic subjective nature of the work—brings to mind Franz Grillparzer's story *Der arme Spielmann*.[41] Very much like the narrator of Grillparzer's *Novelle*, Storm is divided into the role of observer and participant (both Johannes and Storm are artists), and Storm manages to restore a sense of total meaning to life in this way which it would not have as an isolated personal experience. At the same time, however, Storm's objective historical situation forced him to seek meaning where there was none. His literary technique, accordingly, rather resembles the action of the desperate man trying to shore up his continually crumbling defenses against the threat of annihilation by setting up complicated frames and narrative perspectives in order to conceal the basic nihilism of his experience and situation. The effect of *Aquis submersus*, then, is not the one striven for by its author. The dualistic structure of the work—the author's division into a narrator and a character—reflects an esthetic view of tragedy. In such a view, the human condition can only have a pathetic but not a tragic connotation.

III *Eekenhof*

Eekenhof, first published in 1879, is another historical novella. Much like *Aquis submersus*, its story is unearthed by the author-narrator in his native region and pieced together by him. But this time the events themselves are related in the third-person singular.

From the remains of a moat, a giant oak tree, a wooden epitaph in the attic of the village church, depicting the former manor of Eekenhof (Manor Oaks), from local lore and legend, and from "scraps" which the "poets" have gathered here and there for their own purposes, the story of the manor and its last lord is reconstructed. About the picture epitaph the author and narrator says; "And thus it agrees [in its details] with the tale which has been handed down to us." [42] It is the legend of a colonel and a "dark-eyed lady" which, to be sure, is lost in history but whose protagonists the narrator deems important enough to mention, because their fate is said to have been a prefiguration of that of all subsequent generations down to the last owner of *Eekenhof*. Besides this motif of heredity, those of incest and of filicide dominate the main part of the novella.

Squire Hennecke, his father's youngest son, is possessed by selfishness and greed and envies his brother the family estate which, by custom, belongs to the oldest son. As the narrator remarks in a rare aside, "Fortunately there was another way, already established in those days, to acquire property without effort and as if by right of birth; and he applied it twice successfully, so that in later years people were saying that Squire Hennecke was living off two wives, one living and one dead." [43] Thus Hennecke comes to woo a young lady of means, beauty, and sensitivity in contrast to his own coarseness. They are married, and Hennecke becomes the squire of Eekenhof. Soon after having given birth to a sickly boy, Hennecke's wife dies. The boy, hovering between life and death, is entrusted to the care of a relative and regains his health. By law, a son, when he comes of age, will inherit his mother's estate in the absence of any paternal claim to it. Henceforth, Hennecke regards Detlev's existence as a threat to his own, when, twenty years hence, he will have the right to claim his mother's estate. As the years go by, Hennecke decides to protect himself against the day when his son would come of age, and he remarries. Benedikte, his second wife, is well along in years and described as being somewhat of a shrew. She, however, is the owner of a stately manor and sufficient land to disperse any doubts on Hennecke's part. Soon, Benedikte gives birth to two boys, "red-haired" and of stocky build and, as time would reveal, in character very much like their parents. Hennecke's methods of realizing a profit from his estates are cruel and tyrannical. His serfs and all who live near him are afraid of him. The squire spends his time and money on card games and wine. The times are difficult, as the events take place in the second half of the seventeenth century, when Germany was in the aftermath of the devastation of the Thirty Years' War. Against this background, Hennecke's need for a solid economic base, commensurate with his social standing and personal needs, becomes more urgent. While Detlev is in the care of an elderly aunt in the city, Eekenhof is left in the care of an old woman and her granddaughter. Heilwig, as the girl is called, is the daughter of the forester at Manor Oaks. Hennecke, who does not show much affection for his family, cares deeply for Heilwig and becomes clumsy and inarticulate in her presence. Benedikte suspects the real reason for this behavior but is forced to accept the story that nothing is known about Heilwig's father. Whenever she is taken to Hennecke's manor, Heilwig is taunted and tortured by the two boys who call her a cuckoo because of her intrusion into the life of the family and their feeling that she is threatening to take away what is rightfully theirs. After the death of his aunt, Detlev returns to live with his father and his family. Dark-haired and dark-eyed Heilwig, who is as beautiful and gentle as Hennecke's first wife, soon becomes Detlev's inseparable companion and playmate. Detlev, who shuns the company of the two boys, is of sound character and very handsome. He knows that he will inherit Eekenhof, and he promises the serfs and peasants fair and just treatment. Once, when his father had given the order to punish a tenant farmer for disobedience, young Detlev decides to revoke the order because of its cruelty. His father confronts him with his own recalcitrance and strikes Detlev with his riding crop. This incident provides the turning point of the novella. Detlev abruptly leaves his father and goes to sea. As the time of Detlev's maturity approaches and no word has reached his father about his whereabouts, Hennecke has his oldest son declared legally dead. He can now lay claim to the title to Eekenhof.

Upon his twenty-first birthday, however, Detlev returns to claim what is his. He takes certain documents to his father which are to prove his identity and his legal rights to the property, invalidating his father's claims. When he leaves his father's study to go to Eekenhof and see Heilwig, he leaves two pistols behind which he had been carrying. He does not wish to frighten the two women who knew about the circumstances under which he had

left Eekenhof. As Heilwig learns of Detlev's return, it becomes
clear that she has been deeply in love with him ever since their
childhood. Detlev, however, knows about the identity of Heilwig's father and tells her that they are brother and sister.

On the evening of his return, Detlev and Heilwig are sitting in
the "hall of ancestors" under the picture of Detlev's mother. Tired,
both fall asleep in their chairs. They are suddenly awakened by
the presence of an intruder whose startled outcry, moaning, and
swooning cause Detlev to reach for Heilwig and the weapon
which had dropped on the floor when the intruder had fallen.
Detlev recognizes one of his pistols. He and Heilwig flee from the
hall and she whispers "That one meant to kill you!" The narrator
reports that soon rumor had it that Hennecke had been felled that
night by "the shadowy hands" of the woman in the portrait. Soon
afterward, Benedikte dies and Hennecke's son remains legally
dead. Hennecke thus becomes the sole owner of the two estates.
His two sons are now overseeing their mother's estate, and Hennecke lives out his life a broken man. "And thus, in his loneliness,
he reached the outer limit in the life of a man. There was no trace,
however, of Heilwig and the blond horseman [Detlev]." [44]

Eekenhof belongs to a type of Storm-novellas which—very
much like his chronicle novellas—potentially imply an ironic attitude toward the representation of reality. Indeed, it could have
united reader and narrator, in their near-equal distance to the
world represented in the story, to embrace a loftier or more resolute vision of reality. As we have already seen, this would not only
have been alien to Storm's thinking but also contrary to his purpose to involve the reader in his tightly sealed world of fiction,
which represents a defense against a meaningless reality. The all-
important task for Storm was to establish a close personal link
between himself and his material, between his experience and
that of his characters, and between himself and his readers.[45] The
intrusion of the temporary first-person narrator in the frame into
an otherwise objective third-person narrative simply reveals the
author's close connection with his story. The objective narrative
style is merely a disguise for Storm's intense interest in the tragic
events of the story and the fate of his characters. The necessity of
revealing the story gradually from its scattered sources and the
remarks of the narrator to that effect are designed to emphasize
the "reality" of the events. Actually, however, the effect is almost

the opposite of what Storm hoped to achieve. The impact on the reader is one of heightened fictitiousness because the story has never had any place in reality at all, except in the mind of the poet. In the case of *Eekenhof*, where the absence of a manuscript fiction produces the gradualism of the frame, the intent of the author-narrator is clear in two ways. Just as in *Aquis submersus*, the division of the writer into a narrator and an author and the fact that he has an intimate knowledge of his characters' thoughts and actions, belie the apparent objectivity of its style. The motifs already mentioned, therefore, have a personal and private significance. Just as the personal experience alone has meaning for Storm, so does the nature of the type to which this novella belongs confirm its private character. The motifs and the structure serve the underlying theme of transiency and death. The tragic (we would prefer to say "pathetic") determinism of man's existence is what profoundly moves the author and what he wishes the reader to experience as well. The last line of the novella already quoted sounds the basic motif of oblivion and death. It is not an escape into the past (no more so here than in the chronicle novellas) but an attempt to rescue it, to make it "posthumously" a part of the present, an "experience." Hence the author involves himself via the frame and its narrator. In order to make certain that the present is totally assimilated (the present as homeland and family) the past had to be a part of it. Personal suffering alone has meaning, the tragic nature of which must be communicated to the reader.

The use of heredity in *Eekenhof*, expressed in terms of the passing on of good and evil traits which are visited upon the descendants mechanistically, resembles Wulf's and Katharina's situation quite closely. Unlike Wulf in *Aquis submersus*, however, Hennecke has a more sensitive and positive character. It remains undeveloped, however, and he is entirely dominated by the evil in him. Thus, the tragic nature of his situation and of those around him is brought into even greater relief. Yet the very fact of the inevitability of man's condition (symbolized by the gallery of ancestral pictures, the references to the relentless passage of time, the incestual love motif, and the paternal hatred for Detlev) creates a fatalistic mood rather than a profoundly tragic one.

IV *Hans und Heinz Kirch*

This novella is one of the few by Storm written entirely in the disinterested third-person style. Published in 1882, it elicited strong and favorable responses from such extraordinary writers as Keller and Heyse. The story takes place in the small port city of Heiligenhafen on the Baltic Sea where one of Storm's daughters was married to a minister. It was there that Storm learned about the facts underlying his novella, and, in some ways, the episodic character of the novella and its unusual length reflect the anecdotal or chronicle character of its transmission.

The basic theme concerns a conflict between father and son, Hans Kirch and Heinz, as the title read originally. It is, in a way, a repetition of the *culpa patris* theme of *Aquis submersus,* except that this time there can be no doubt about the father's guilt. Storm's strong interest in the theme stemmed from his own tragic experience with his oldest son, Hans. Storm chose to treat the conflict as a fateful constellation rather than as a psychologically motivated struggle between father and son. The novella spans the life of Heinz Kirch from his birth to his death and his father's rise and old age. Story and plot, however, concentrate entirely upon the relationship of the two, with Hans Kirch being the actual protagonist. The story is set in the small Baltic harbor town where Hans Kirch is the captain of a small merchantman. The narrator describes it as contemporary and middle class whose business is business. The focal points in the lives of its seafaring and church-going citizens are the "Bürgerglocke" (citizen's bell), which strikes at ten o'clock every evening to remind the young to return home, and the "Schifferstuhl" (captain's pew) in the medieval church. The accepted path to respectability for a young man would lead him from "cabin boy and captain on a family or personally owned ship to becoming shipowner and senator in the town council; such was the hierarchical progress of middle-class respectability," the narrator concludes.[46] About the segregated and elevated pew in the church, the narrator has this to say:

It is understandable that upon entering the church many a young sailor or helmsman from the petty bourgeoisie would be overcome not by devotion but by an ambitious desire to gain admission to that place up there, and that then—despite the forceful sermon—he would return

to his ship or his quarters with worldly resolve instead of divine in-
spiration.[47]

With the same irony the author proceeds to characterize Hans
Kirch as a man of patience, thrift, and hard work embodying the
ideals typical of his social class and environment. Kirch, who had
risen from the "petty bourgoisie" to the position of shipowner and
representative in the town council, is a man devoted to his career
and family. There is, however, a tragic flaw in his character, his
irascibility which ultimately proves the undoing of both father
and son. Soon after Heinz's sixth birthday, his father takes him
on his first voyage. While he is taking a nap below, the small child
ventures out on the ship's bowsprit. After much anxiety, the boy
finds his way back from his perilous position. Hans Kirch's anguish turns into sudden anger, and he says to the boy "Don't ever
do that to me again!" With that, he turns on the cabin boy who
happens to be near and punishes him severely. The incident
makes a deep impression on young Heinz, and it represents the
first serious breach in the relationship between father and son, as
well as being a turning point in the plot. From then on, the boy
shows increasing signs of resentment, fear, and independence
from his father. The mother, who is a minor figure in the story,
cannot heal the rift. As the years pass, it is said of Hans Kirch that
his love for Heinz became less and less evident "the more the
boy's own will grew; indeed, he himself believed that he loved his
son only as the beneficiary of his ambitious plans." [48]

At this point, another character is introduced. It is a small girl
called Wieb, the illegitimate child of a sailor and a washerwoman
who now lives with another man. Wieb is a typical Stormian female character who, like Elisabeth in *Immensee*, is beautiful, of
high moral character, and weak, making her entirely the victim of
circumstances. In lyrical language, the narrator describes the
childhood idyl in which Heinz acts as the protector and constant
companion of the younger girl. All of his pent-up tenderness and
love is showered on her, causing her to feel eternal gratitude and
love. On his seventeenth birthday, Heinz, according to custom, is
going to spend one year at sea as a seaman's apprentice. On the
evening of his departure, Heinz and Wieb steal away to an
amusement park. There, in a scene reminiscent of Keller's *Romeo*

und Julia auf dem Dorfe, Heinz buys Wieb a ring which she puts on a string around his neck as a pledge of trust.

Hans Kirch's sister, the town gossip, relates to her brother the story of the young lovers who had been seen together. Wieb's family background is considered to be detrimental to Kirch's plans for his son, because they involve no less than the accumulation of sufficient wealth to be accepted by the patrician families. In order to become a senator, it is necessary to belong to the class of established wealth. Kirch hopes to make it possible for his son to become a senator. Again, he is completely overwhelmed by rage and writes an abusive letter to Heinz, forbidding him to continue his relationship with Wieb. Heinz does not reply, nor does he return at the end of his year at sea. Instead, he takes service on another ship. The son's refusal to return home turns into a contest of wills, and the father interprets it in this way. Hans Kirch expects his son to make the first move, in keeping with the Fourth Commandment. At the end of two years, a letter arrives with many foreign postmarks and marked "postage due." When father Kirch is handed the letter, he refuses to accept it. He is furious that his son cannot even afford the thirty shillings for postage. "Scoundrel!, he shouted, you will not enter your father's house like this!" [49] The letter is returned to Heinz unopened. Wieb, who had seen the postman with the letter, begs in vain to be allowed to pay for it.

The rejection of his son incurs his first real guilt. Heinz's mother, who has never spoken a harsh word and suffered quietly, is moved to rebellion: "Hans! Hans! to do that without me was not right! Now we can only pray that the letter is not returned to its author; but God will not burden you with such serious guilt." [50]

After a caesura of fifteen years, the narrator remarks, again ironically, that there is not much that has changed for the town and its people. The citizen's bell continues to toll at the same hour for the youthful stragglers, reminding them to return home. The year is 1871, the post office is now called the "Imperial Mail," and the city's senators are titled "councilors," reflecting the rule of the Prussian administration. After the mother's death and the appearance of another minor character, Lina, Heinz Kirch's sister, the story resumes at the beginning of the seventeenth year after the son's disappearance. Rumor has it that a man answering to the name of John Smidt was seen in a cheap boardinghouse in Hamburg. It is almost certain that this man is Heinz Kirch. Lina's husband points out to her that her enthusiasm was premature, because her brother's return would alter their situation rather radically, since Heinz would now inherit his father's business. This time, Hans Kirch decides to look for his son and bring him home. When the two return, Heinz's appearance is quite different from what the family remembered. There are scars on his face, and his manner seems coarse and unfamiliar. His speech is punctuated with English and Spanish phrases, and it is discovered that the anchor tattooed on his arm has disappeared. The ensuing days and weeks produce no closeness among the family members, and the conversations with Heinz are monosyllabic. Only once is the subject of the letter brought up between father and son, but no reconciliation is effected. Soon, new rumors circulate to the effect that the person living in Captain Kirch's house is not his son. The Kirch family secretly welcomes this opportunity for disavowing this obvious failure in their midst of probably doubtful origin. Thus, after Heinz is seen in a disreputable tavern in town and does not return home until early morning, the father impatiently and forcefully tells him to leave his house. Later that day, the father leaves an envelope with a modest sum of money in his son's room.

The events leading to this second rejection of the son by the father are preceded by Heinz's return to Wieb, a signal that the middle-aged man is indeed Heinz Kirch. Wieb is now the wife of a sailor and lives with her stepfather who owns a disreputable tavern in town. The very sentimental recognition scene in the tavern culminates in Wieb's lacrimose admission that the past must be forever buried and that she is no longer free to marry him. Heinz takes off the ring from around his neck and throws it down. This symbolic gesture removes any doubt which the reader might have harbored about his identity and directly signals the end of any ties which had bound him to this town. The father decides that Heinz's presence in the tavern, which had been duly reported to him, was the definite sign of his son's lack of respectability. Heinz removes a small amount from the envelope and appends a brief message on the back of it, in English. "Thanks for the alms and farewell for ever." [51]

On a stormy night some time after Heinz's departure, the father has a vision of his son's death at sea. He believes in his premonition. The story closes with a rather unlikely scene which shows the rapidly aging Kirch on the town's pier in the company of Wieb. The visionary experience is said to have changed the father completely, and he is now utterly distraught and convinced of his own guilt. He, therefore, accepts Wieb's company as an act of belated atonement for the injustices committed against his son. She is, posthumously, the daughter-in-law of a dying old man and a dead son, and he even remembers her in his will. His death, his son-in-law's succession to his fortune, the arrival of a grandson, and his father's prospects to be elected senator are the concluding events, listed laconically, and only one question remains unanswered—"but where is Heinz Kirch?" [52]

The adventurous character of the son and the rigidity of the father account for the two characters' inability to compromise. With inexorable logic, the cruelty of the father and the suffering of the son lead to a tragic conclusion. As has been pointed out, the conflict between father and son alone would not have been sufficient to motivate the tragic events. They are exclusively the father's fault. His stubbornness and irascibility lie at the heart of the problem. [53] As Storm himself commented, "he sins and he atones!" Nevertheless, and not too surprisingly, there are several factors which tend to obscure the issue of crime and punishment and, hence, of genuine tragedy. In spite of the objective third-person perspective, the narrative shows several structural weaknesses which betray not only the author's emotional involvement but also his determination to tone down what may seem utterly irreconcilable, namely, the world as it is and the world as it ought to be. For whatever guilt the father incurs by the rejection of his son—in fact, the narrator likens the refusal to pay the thirty shillings to the betrayal of Christ—he is the product of his social milieu, even in respect to his strictness. The ironic stance of the narrator to this narrow-minded town represents an even stronger indictment than the sins of omission of Hans Kirch. Theodor Storm wrote to Erich Schmidt, the young Germanist: "The old man is not too harsh, our people here are like that; only I should have written another scene in which paternal love would have been visible which, of course, had been lying dormant in him all along." [54]

This ironic narrative attitude toward narrow-mindedness and greed is uncommon in Storm's work. To be sure, his correspond-

ence and some of his political poetry are filled with bitterness and
sarcasm about the political and social status quo of the era of
Bismarck. The ironic stance, however, does not go so far as taking
the form of a direct address to the reader, in the manner of, say,
Dostoevsky's novels. A total and irreconcilable conflict is not portrayed in the novella. The contradictions and antinomies of human existence, in the last analysis, are not resolved by reflection.
Rather, Storm seeks reconciliation by either a fatalistic acceptance
of the inevitable, as in his early works, or he struggles to find a
transcendental solution, as in *Hans und Heinz Kirch* and in *Der
Schimmelreiter*. The lyrical passages of the novella chiefly exist in
order to protect the tragic core, which consists essentially of two
elements, namely, the transitoriness of youth, love, and innocence
(or simply of life), and the tragic conflict between father and son,
which is ordained by fate and circumstance. The final scene between the old man, Wieb, and the "social democrat" serves to cast
light upon the author's intent. Hans Kirch says " 'He is dead . . . I
know it for certain; but—in eternity, I shall know my Heinz
again.' 'Yes,' she replied, 'in eternity.' " To the disreputable carpenter, whom the townspeople call the "social democrat" and who
interrupts Hans Kirch with the question "What is eternity to us
humans?," he now replies, "Don't you know who I am, Jürgen
Hans? . . . I am Hans Kirch who rejected his son twice! Do you
hear me, Jürgen Hans? Twice I rejected my Heinz, and for that
reason my concern is with eternity!" The skeptical Jürgen of
whom the narrator says that he thought he had discovered a loop-
hole in his Christian faith, and who was now determined to argue
with others about it "as small minds are wont to do," is quick to
respond in very unbiblical language (in contrast to Hans Kirch)
"I am sorry, Mr. Kirch, . . . but eternity is only in the heads of
old women!" [55] It is characteristic of Storm that he leaves the answer open. Neither the rationalistic skepticism (which largely corresponds to Storm's personal viewpoint in religious matters) nor
the visionary Hans Kirch's belief in reconciliation and forgiveness
in eternity is held to be absolute truth. The ironic description of
the carpenter implies a critical distance from his point of view as
well, and Hans Kirch's visionary experience points only to a possible answer to the question. But the narrator knows that if a reconciliation is possible at all, it will be so only in eternity or never.
What is tragic is the fact that life could not resolve the conflict but

only death could. He says of the old father after the latter's change of heart: "The dead man now had all the rights which he had denied to the living." [56]

Because Storm wants to protect the basically tragic view of life expressed in the narrative he avoids the irreconcilable conflict, the unbreachable gap between reality and experience. The "lyrical" and, indeed, sentimental passages are a subconscious device to protect the subjective from the "real" lest it destroy the hard-won gains of a harmonious world view. As we have said earlier, the conflict between reality and illusion, or the subjective and the objective, in Storm, already points toward the absolute subjectivism of the Symbolists and Impressionists. It is, therefore, paradoxically, these stylistically weak passages which lend to Storm a modern appeal rather than the "realistically portrayed tragic conflict between father and son." Meaning can lie in a reality which no amount of objectivity can grasp. Storm and many other writers of his time were aware of that fact. Storm struggled to overcome his hopelessness by employing the topos of the supernatural and by using his lyrical approach to some of the problems of life.[57] Perhaps one of the most poorly motivated parts of the novella is the final scene between Wieb and Heinz. Why did he not write to her, one might ask, and why the belated declaration of love? Equally saccharine is the final passage when the old man and Wieb have found each other. As Benno von Wiese remarks, it is a conciliatory gesture to tone down the harshness of the father's personality and guilt.[58] He is described as a feeble man with trembling hands given to lacrimose self-recrimination while Wieb merely assents to all he says and does. Again, however, it is evanescence which seems tragic to Storm, and this experience is expressed here, however poorly motivated. "I hate having to motivate!" Storm was wont to say.

This tendency to protect the subjective world view from outside peril excludes a totally ironic narrative attitude. What has been said of the *Biedermeier* poet Adalbert Stifter in this connection applies to Storm as well: "Through a well-developed system of frame tales, he more and more screens off the tragic core and thus arrives at the form of the novel." [59] In fact, in Storm too there is a tendency toward the length and episodic style of the novel which simply remains unrealized. *Hans und Heinz Kirch,* then, despite its apparently objective point of view, betrays, by its structure, the personal involvement of its author and his fear of losing his readers and its meaning unless the starkly tragic events were cast in the gentle glow of pathos.

V   A Chapter in the History of Grieshuus

Similar to *Eekenhof* and *Aquis submersus,* this novella too is gradually pieced together from remaining "evidence." It is a historical novella, a drama of life and death and oblivion or a "Romantic novella" as Storm called it in his diary.[60] First published in 1884, this lyrical chronicle is one of the most voluminous among his novellas. Again, while it cannot be called a novel, it exhibits balladlike traits[61] and has an episodic structure. As Storm wrote to Keller, "I am losing myself amongst the trees and heather of bygone times, and I am letting Boccaccio's falcon fly where it may." [62]

Typologically, *Zur Chronik von Grieshuus* represents a different form among Storm's chronicles. Its frame tale and the first part of the actual narrative are related by the author-narrator in the first-person singular, and the second part of the novella is told by a minor character in the story. The time is the Thirty Years' War, and the action of Book II takes place in the eighteenth century. The major motifs of the story are love, fratricide, and atonement. The leading motif, however, around which—like an axis—move all its parts and episodes, is that of transiency and oblivion. It is this motif which Storm had in mind when he defended himself against Fontane's criticism that the novella consisted of isolated scenes loosely strung together.[63]

During his last year in the school of his native town (apparently Husum), the narrator discovers his interest in the fate of the erstwhile owners of Grieshuus Manor. On his excursions to the surrounding countryside he comes upon the ruins of the former estate and proceeds to reconstruct its history for the reader, calling himself jokingly "the chronicler of Grieshuus" whose notes are beginning to fill the copybook he has started. The narrator now proceeds to assemble these notes half a century later by way of an obvious reference to Storm's age at the actual time of writing; that is, at the time of the discovery of the story he was seventeen, and at the time of writing, in 1883, sixty-six. This attempt at affirming the veracity of his fiction merely tends to emphasize the author's close involvement with his story. In a way, the reference to him-

self also prefigures the leading motif of time (or transiency)
which is to indicate the passage of time since the narrator came
upon the fragments of his story. In keeping with his attempts to
justify his fictitious historical tale, the narrator proceeds to relate
the events in the objective style of the third-person singular. The
events concern the last squire of Grieshuus, Hinrich, and his
younger brother Detlev as well as their father. As in *Hans und
Heinz Kirch*, irascibility is a family trait which leads to violence
and tragedy. The older brother is described as practical-minded
whereas the younger one has the mind of a diplomat and scholar.
Both have narrow eyes and prominent noses, and Hinrich's bad
temper expresses itself through his "flashing eyes." Not only as the
oldest son but also by his interests and practical nature, Hinrich
seems destined to become the future master of the estate. Hinrich's penchant for violence is brought out by an episode in which
he attacks one of his serfs with a club for an act of negligence.
Later, in a fit of rage, he kills his hunting dog. Both times Hinrich
has pangs of remorse. As the years pass, his younger brother
Detlev enters the service of the Duke of Schleswig. At this point,
the narrator comments that the bell was to toll for Hinrich, "a
fateful one, announcing the final hour of the house of Grieshuus." [64] Subsequently a minor character is introduced, Bärbe,
the daughter of a former serf at Grieshuus, who has moved with
her father, a scribe, to the estate. Hinrich and Bärbe fall in
love with each other. A typical Stormian female character, she is
gentle and very reticent, providing a sharp contrast to Hinrich's ill
temper. The ensuing events are related against the backdrop of the
Polish wars which now disrupt the peaceful lives of the inhabi-
tants of Grieshuus. Marauding bands of soldiers make the countryside unsafe, and Hinrich becomes the protector of Bärbe and
her father. The love scenes are purely lyrical and similar in function and style to those of *Hans und Heinz Kirch*. Once, when
Bärbe tries to kill a chicken to make broth for her ailing father,
Hinrich has to take her place, for she cannot do it. By way of a
confession, Hinrich tells her about the dog he once killed. He
must promise her never again to kill, and he replies: "Mark my
word, I promise it!" [65]

The conflict which now develops is caused by Bärbe's inferior
social status. Hinrich's father forbids him to marry a commoner.
The chaotic events of the war accompany the plot as in carefully

orchestrated music, prefiguring a sad outcome. Before his death, and contrary to custom, the father bequeaths the estate to Detlev, because he is unable to dissuade Hinrich and Bärbe from marriage. Detlev's arrogance, the father's rigidity, and Hinrich's irascibility must inevitably lead to a tragic outcome. One year after their marriage, Bärbe gives birth to a seven-month baby, a girl. During her convalescence, a letter from Detlev arrives, stating that his brother's marriage was legally null and void. Since Detlev was the rightful heir to Grieshuus and since Bärbe's status as a free person had never been made official, he should have been consulted. As the owner of Grieshuus and of all serfs within the purview of the estate, he refuses to consent to their marriage. This was Detlev's carefully contrived revenge for his brother's usurpation of the estate. Since Detlev had no real interest in his father's inheritance and did not live there either, Hinrich had tacitly assumed unofficial title to the estate. In her weakened physical state this news so frightens and upsets Bärbe that it precipitates her death. When Hinrich learns of this event he fights a duel with his brother, in the course of which Detlev is slain. Thus, at the end of Book I the narrator and author concludes, "in the mansion lay a beautiful but dead wife and next to her in the cradle a seven-month baby, a girl. Such was the state of the heirs of Grieshuus." [66]

At this juncture, the narrator purports to have come upon an eighteenth-century manuscript by the hand of a Master Caspar Bokenfeld, tutor to the last descendant of the squire of Grieshuus. Book II, then, represents the fictitious firsthand account of this minor character. Soon after the murder Hinrich disappears from Grieshuus leaving his baby girl in the care of a distant relative and the estate in the care of a trusted servant. The killing, which had taken place on the twenty-fourth of January, remains in the memory of the people as an uncanny event which has been followed ever since by the "evil days" on each anniversary of the day. Bokenfeld's account resumes with the beginning of the eighteenth century, that is, more than a generation after the tragic events have taken place. After turning away many a suitor with the words "I must wait for the return of my father, so he can give me away properly," Hinrich's daughter finally gives up all hope and marries a Swedish colonel whom the events of yet another war had swept into the vicinity of Grieshuus. From this marriage springs a child, a boy called Rolf. His mother does not survive his birth, and he grows up at Grieshuus in the care of his father and an aunt. In order to cope with the wolves that have begun to roam the forests of the estate, the Colonel hires an old man who comes highly recommended as a hunter. The hunter's identity is clear to the reader the moment he accepts his position upon the condition that he be permitted to move into the mansion once a year during "the evil days." With some difficulty the relationship between Rolf and the hunter develops into one of love as between father and son. Only the old servants who once knew Hinrich suspect the identity of the old hunter. One evening, the squire is about to lure the last of the wolves into a trap and asks Rolf to spring it. That night the old man reveals himself to Rolf as his grandfather, with the ubiquitous narrator, Master Bokenfeld, nearby.

By way of echoing the love motif of the first part of the story, a young girl named Abel, a commoner living at Grieshuus, falls in love with Rolf, who is now a young man. He does not return her feelings, however, and eventually she marries the tutor. With the killing of the last wolf, the hunter's mission had come to its end, and he takes his leave. Rolf enters the Swedish army where he serves as an officer. During the war between the Swedes and the Russians, Rolf's squadron has entered the territory of his former home. The news of his arrival in the vicinity is greeted with great expectation. The date is the ominous twenty-fourth of January. Instead of Rolf, however, Abel and the old hunter arrive to bring news of an imminent attack by the Russians upon the Swedes near Grieshuus. It is decided to warn Rolf and his Swedish defenders. The hunter volunteers to carry the message since the servants cannot be persuaded to leave the estate during the "evil days." That night Rolf is killed in battle, and the body of the hunter is found dead the next morning. The bodies lie in state, and the coffins are placed side by side in the mansion. The Colonel, who has learned the story of squire Hinrich from one of the servants, now eulogizes their death before the assembled household:

Listen! Not I and not my son whom Lord God has taken away from me—but the old man here in the second coffin was your master until the end. But you did not see him, and when he came as a servant, you did not recognize him; he remained restless and a fugitive all his life according to the curse of the scriptures, because he had slain his brother in a fit of rage. But not as Cain slew Abel: the brother had destroyed his all, his young wife, and so he forced him to a fight and killed him. . . .[67]

After the burial, the Colonel has the crypt sealed with a brick wall and leaves Grieshuus forever. The narrator's marriage to Abel and his report about the deterioration of the estate, the crumbling walls, and the cutting of the giant oaks in the Grieshuus forest conclude the second part of the novella.

Essentially *Zur Chronik von Grieshuus* deals with two themes just as it consists of two distinct parts. In the first part it is the theme of fratricidal conflict which dominates the plot, and in the second the expiation of Hinrich's guilt. As we have already mentioned, the unifying element must be seen in the old Stormian motif of transiency. It is this motif, and the concept of tragedy developed from it, which account for the structure, style, and leitmotifs of the tale.

The atmosphere of a legend which pervades the story establishes a much closer link between the author and his material than even the narrative perspective would indicate. The allusion to the "Nordic Saga Atmosphere" which lured the narrator to the former site of Grieshuus determines its style and tone. In keeping with the legendary character of the story, the author employs the supernatural aspect, lyrical passages, and leitmotifs to amplify the leading motif of transiency and obliteration. It is thus not the legend of Squire Hinrich and the decline and fall of his family, but the tragedy of the transitoriness of existence. It is this aspect which moves the author and narrator profoundly and which he wishes to convey to the reader. This may also be the reason why Storm did not consistently adhere to the structural demands of his novella. He sets the mood in the opening frame by alluding to the atmosphere of the landscape, the ruins of Grieshuus, the superstitions which have sprung from the murderous conflict. These are the reasons which account for the fragmentary character of the story. Therefore, the contemporary narrator is obliged to introduce his account with such phrases as ". . . it is said that . . . ," ". . . it is not known whether . . . ," ". . . not much is known but . . ." and the like. Gradually, however, he forgoes all pretense at uncertainty and even lapses into an archaic style, approximating the language of the seventeenth century. He does so in order to give free play to the atmospheric impact of the events but does not bother to justify the "Baroque" style by introducing another source or narrator for it.

At the end of the first part, the author-narrator interrupts the course of events to introduce the minor character of Master Bokenfeld who is to tell the remainder of the story. Again, Storm is forced to manipulate his material in an unconvincing way (i.e., by introducing the manuscript fiction of the tutor), in order to recount the other half of the story from the proper vantage point. Since the second part required an intimate knowledge of the characters and their motivations, he used a character-narrator. Rolf's mother, Hinrich's daughter, dies after childbirth, and, in time, the father hires a tutor for the boy: "Thus Master Bokenfeld came to be at the estate, and with him a man to whom I can leave the narration from now on in his own name." [68] Moreover, the elements of the second book—Hinrich's atonement and his acquisition of self-discipline—needed the sympathetic treatment by this minor but keen and understanding observer. Storm relates to this narrator in a rather cool and distant manner in order to direct the reader's attention to the crucial points of his narrative. For example, Master Bokenfeld, who aspires to the ministry, is told by the colonel when one of the slain wolves is brought in for inspection, "where are the clergy? They too like to feast their eyes upon the vanquished enemy!" [69] On the other hand, sentimental passages such as the following, go uncensored. Having introduced the character of Rolf, the narrator is moved to say in anticipation, "My Rolf, my beautiful boy, just why did the Lord call for you so soon!" At the very end of the novella—and without reintroducing the narrator of the frame—the tutor quotes from "a poet" to give expression to his sentiment: "Such is the world, as the poet sings, 'Nothing lasts on earth, it must perish / Death comes, you cannot conquer it. / For a while someone might remember you; / Then you are swept away, and the broom goes on sweeping!' " [70]

Aside from these considerations of style and narrative perspective, the lyrical quality of the story requires some comment. As has already been mentioned, the author employs two devices (in addition to the leading motif of transiency) to achieve his desired effect of a nostalgic atmosphere of reminiscence, the leitmotif and the symbol.

There are two leitmotifs which accompany the composition: heredity and chaos. The motif of heredity in this novella is treated both biologically and mythically. The trait of irascibility inherited from the father down to his two sons and his great-grandson Rolf, and the instinctive love of the hunter for him are the recurring expressions of this motif. Even the manifestation of this trait is repeated by Rolf, that is, Hinrich's attempt to kill his hound, except that the hunter stays his hand, saying "Don't, you might do that to a man some day!" [71] But the accent does not primarily lie on the tragedy of heredity as inescapable fact and fate. Therefore the negative influences can be checked. Thus Hinrich says to Rolf after the incident with his dog, "It is your blood, my child, we must know against what we are fighting!" [72]

The leitmotif of chaos is produced by the war which accompanies the action. It is the vagaries and fortunes of war which bring the Colonel to Grieshuus and into the lives of its surviving members, the daughter of Hinrich and their son. The dedication of the new gallows in town, the public revelry that follows, and the deaths of Hinrich and Rolf are foreshadowed by a reference to the Polish wars ("Polackenkrieg") with all its attendant horrors. Above all, however, it is the recurring motif of the wolves roaming in the neglected forest of the estate as a result of the war among the brothers—much like the war being waged on the outside—which underscores and echoes, in the manner of a musical theme, the chaotic events: "The wolf, the grisly dog," the people say; and Matten, the old caretaker woman, never tires of saying "Trust the Lord." Both are expressions of fear caused by the chaotic state of the world.

Closely connected with these motifs is the symbolic significance of the union and interdependency of man and nature and the twenty-fourth of January, the day of Detlev's death. The date is transformed into an event of supernatural significance. The people of the area, including the hunter, believe in the "evil days" on which an evil spirit, the ghost of the slain squire, seeks to strangle a victim for revenge. Thus old Matten goes to church during those days, and the old hunter stays in the mansion. Indeed, the hunter, offering his services, arrives on the second Sunday after Epiphany, heralding the "evil days" which not only conjure up the death of Detlev but also prefigure the violent deaths of the remaining male members of the house of Grieshuus. Further, as has been observed before,[73] the date alludes to another famous one in the history of German literature, the *Twenty-Fourth of February* by Zacharias Werner, a tragedy of fate. In the case of Storm's novella, however, it is not blind fate that rules the lives of the characters, but they are governed by personal guilt, supernatural powers, and a mechanistic hereditary force. The superstitious beliefs and the visionary element (Matten's prescience) are really symbolic projections of the events which tend to give them significance beyond themselves, without forcing the narrator to give up his neutral attitude. A symbolic link is established even between the last of the wolves with her brood and Bärbe's premature baby by justifying the animal's death, because, unlike the squire's wife, the she-wolf had already given birth.

The point at which the leitmotifs and symbols converge is the supernatural and the role it plays in all Storm's novellas. At the beginning of the first part, as well as at the end, the narrative perspective shifts to a vantage point which casts doubt on the causality of the events. In both instances, it is a prescient quality which makes fate more than a mechanical chain of cause and effect. The narrator of the frame tale tells us that "a superstition hovered over this heath, the last shadow of a sinister human fate with which an old family had vanished from the earth. A time of year is said to exist, or to have existed, when he who traversed this valley after sunset would suffer a horrible fate which blunted the very powers of his life, if not exterminating them." [74] Similarly, the death of Detlev is depicted from the point of view of a young girl—Matten in her youth—endowed with a certain prophetic gift ("Vorspuk") which enables her to presage dire happenings. She not only forecasts Detlev's death but also the dire consequences of the murder for the squire's family and his descendants.

It should be noted that the supernatural occurrences are reported with the skepticism befitting a man of learning. Master Bokenfeld discredits Matten's talk as old wives' tales and gossip among the servants. He listens and calls such talk "Phantasmata" (phantasies) but prefers to keep his thoughts to himself.[75] Thus, while not committing himself, the poet at least holds out the possibility of a transcendental perspective on human fate for which the legend of Grieshuus offers an example. This aspect of the novella contrasts notably with its abstract concept of time, that is to say, with the strait jacket of a plot line or chronology whose progression is measured in calendar and clock time rather than in concrete terms based on subjective experience.

We have said that transiency is the story's leading motif about which group themselves, as around an axis, all remaining motifs. Paradoxically, however, transiency also functions antithetically here, in so far as it is the manifestation of a subjective view of the world. As such, it is in opposition to the realistic style of the story which consists of an implicit concept of continuity (i.e., an illusion of continuity) by virtue of its historico-chronological frame, that is, a realistic setting which is to contain precisely the forces which actually elude it, namely those of transiency.[76] Therein lies a contradiction inherent in all of Storm's "chronicle" novellas. The illusion of an objective reality in terms of a nexus of continuity contrasts with an entirely subjective concept of transiency, at one point dividing or breaking the axis of transiency, so to speak, and thereby giving the work a bipolar structure.

The potential for a higher meaning to life lies, as already noted, in the supernatural or the "poetic" as Storm himself called it. Perhaps this transcendental potential represents a step forward from the escapist attitude which characterized Storm's earlier production and which is reflected in this passage from a letter to his father-in-law of 1866: "Since her death [Constanze's] the feeling of the transitoriness of life has become so powerful and domineering in me that, because of it, the concentration, the warm and secure contemplation of life, without which no poesy is thinkable, has become impossible." [77]

VI   A Festival at Haderslevhuus

This novella was first published in 1885 in a literary magazine, bearing the title *Another Lembeck* (*Noch ein Lembeck*). Its publication led to some serious but constructive criticism, most notably by Storm's friend Heyse, and resulted in a second version of the story. In the original version, the familiar author-narrator of the frame tale draws upon historical sources as well as on his own memory. The source for the latter, so the narrator pretends, was a rare book which is no longer available but which he had once read in his youth.

Since the work concerns a love story similar to the Tristan and Isolde legend, Storm changed the title to its present form to indicate the central event, the love-death scene at Haderslevhuus at the end of the story. He also shortened the introductory part in order to refer directly to the extant historical sources for his narrative (the Lembecks were an old Schleswig-Holstein family) and freely admits to the fictitious nature of his tale—reminiscent of the medieval courtly epic: "[Rolf Lembeck] is not mentioned by the chroniclers . . . I, however, know of him; and of what I know, I feel the urge to speak today." [78] The medieval romance is told in slightly antiquated style which caused Storm inadvertently to slip into the iambic meter in the love scenes between Dagmar and Rolf. In this, too, he willingly accepted Heyse's critical advice and rewrote these passages in ordinary prose. The revised edition of the novella appeared in book form a few months after the first. Early in 1886, it was published together with the other chronicle novellas under the title *Long Ago (Vor Zeiten)*.

While Storm had accepted Heyse's criticism, he rejected Wilhelm Petersen's critique that he had produced no more than a historical novella in the style of a genre popular at the time. On December 12, 1885, Storm replied:

1. If, in a work of art, the representation of past customs and manners is the essential point, then its validity depends upon contemporary trends, or better yet: upon current fashion. If the essence is the representation of the purely human, the timeless, then current trends cannot dilute it, and such modest use of historical trappings as is made here cannot destroy it. On the other hand, what is there in the feelings of my characters that the people of the fourteenth century would have experienced in a different way? 2. What is wrong in having portrayed a sixteen-year-old girl as a lover? The choice resulted almost with necessity from the material. Goethe's Mignon is even younger. If I have rendered only a mediocre portrait, then you are right, to be sure. . . . I do not argue against your rejection of my work, but against your reasons. Incidentally, I have made some rather careful studies. The essential part of it is probably correct.[79]

The argument of the "purely human and timeless" is essentially the same as the one Storm had used in the defense of his fairy tales. Again, one would concede that the historical novellas, like the fairy tales, do not simply constitute an escape into the past from unpleasant contemporary reality. Rather, the quest for a profound meaning to life continues to occupy the poet. Of course, to plead the general humanity of the story as the reason for its being, is no more than an allegorization. Contributing to the dilemma is the fact that Storm here had turned to material which reflected the contemporary interest in Germanic mythology and the preference for the monumental characteristic of that imperialistic age. Also, the love story is once more Storm's way of sharing a discovery with his readers, namely that nothing lasts, that all must perish. Thus, at the end of the story, the narrator quotes a verse from the *Lay of the Nibelungen:* "Even love brings sorrow in the end!"

The plot concerns an event in the lives of three persons belonging to two families. The Lembecks, squires of Schleswig-Holstein, alternately loyal to the Danish king and to the Duke of Schleswig, are at war with King Waldemar of Denmark when the story opens. The hero of the story, Rolf Lembeck, after completing his education in the liberal arts and the courtly virtues in Paris and in Prague, returns home to Dorning, the family castle. Rolf, who is not only of sterling character but also very handsome, is destined to become the master of Dorning, because his father has decided to build a stronghold against Waldemar on the island of Föhr. After Rolf's return, the father selects a candidate from among the eligible maidens to become his wife. Wulfhild, a widow, beautiful, well-to-do, and a descendant of the house of Schauenburg, counts of Holstein, is the father's choice. She is strong-willed and sensuous. The Lembecks do not know that she had poisoned her first husband as an act of revenge for his infidelity. Rolf's handsome appearance and Wulfhild's sensuous beauty prove irresistible to both and rapidly lead to their betrothal, much to the elder Lembeck's satisfaction. The conflict basic to the novella arises from Wulfhild's character demanding absolute loyalty and Rolf's idealistic nature. Thus their marriage is chiefly based on a concept of "low courtly love" and soon leaves Rolf unfulfilled and dissatisfied. He is, therefore, more than willing to follow his inclination and seek an all-encompassing love. When he hears Dagmar's voice and contrives to meet her, he falls deeply in love with her. She is the young daughter of the neighboring representative of the Danish king at Haderslevhuus Castle, Hans Ravenstrupp. Dagmar, barely a woman and of delicate health, is, next to her father, the only survivor of her family, which had fallen victim to the plague. Rolf appears to her as a knight-errant whose true identity she does not know. Wulfhild, having become suspicious of her husband's frequent absences, delegates a faithful servant, Gaspard the Scribe, to spy on Rolf. Her discovery of Rolf's infidelity coincides with his discovery of her as the murderess of her first husband. With the help of Gaspard, Wulfhild contrives to have Rolf sent to his father in order to separate him from Dagmar and to tell her father to intervene. Rolf Lembeck, at the same time, wants to seek his father's counsel to annul his marriage, so he can marry Dagmar. He is, therefore, quite in accord with his father's request to visit him at Föhr. During Rolf's absence Wulfhild reveals to Hans Ravenstrupp what had been going on between his daughter and her husband. The king's man has the giant poplar cut down which straddled the wall and the castle garden and which served Rolf as a secret entrance. This incident and the father's revelation that her lover is a married man so excite and upset his daughter that she dies. Hans Ravenstrupp vows to avenge her death and gives orders that it be kept secret for three days. In the meantime, Wulfhild has learned that her murderous act has become known and abruptly leaves Dorning to go into hiding. Rolf, after his return from Föhr, receives an invitation to a "wedding" at Haderslevhuus. He is led to believe that Dagmar's father has decided to give away his daughter in marriage to a man of his choice. The wedding turns out to be a wake, and when the open coffin is carried to the chapel, Rolf, in extreme despair, seizes the body and, pursued by Ravenstrupp's men, escapes into the tower of the castle. At the top of the tower Rolf is pursued by the father and runs to the parapet. Before he can reach him, Rolf, with Dagmar's body in his arms, jumps from the tower to meet his death. The story concludes with a somber question: "'And the others?' you ask, 'what became of them?' . . . What does it matter? The echo of their footsteps has not sounded in centuries and will never be heard again." [80]

As Franz Stuckert points out, the three main characters represent—aside from their literary function—three strata of medieval life. Wulfhild is a character fashioned after the primitive and demonic Brunhild of the pagan Nibelungen epic, and Dagmar is the *anima candida* (as she is called in the story) of medieval Christian mysticism. The Augustinian dualism of the *civis dei* and the *civis diaboli* is alluded to in the description of Dagmar's fascination with the courtly legend of *Der arme Heinrich* by Hartmann von Aue. Her willingness to sacrifice her life to save the life of the worldly knight corresponds to an aspect of hers and Rolf's character. When they meet for the first time, they recite to each other parts of dialogue from Gottfried von Strassburg's *Tristan und Isolt,* the courtly epic bearing the greatest resemblance to their own story of absolute love and devotion whose all-consuming power can be satisfied only in common death.

Aside from the already discussed use of a first-person narrator, Storm employs another narrative device which comes close to constituting an ironic narrative perspective. The "scenic" structure of this novella, where the action shifts from one locale to the other without adhering to a sequence of time and place but indicating simultaneity, tends to make it more open-ended. This tendency is supported by the occasional remarks of the narrator and by Gaspard with the effect of anticipating the course of events. The reader's attention, therefore, tends to be focused to a larger extent upon the motives for the character's actions as well as upon the symbolism of the tragedy than on the suspense created by the mysteries of an unfamiliar plot. Gaspard, Wulfhild's trusted servant and scribe, is half sage and half fool, thereby achieving not only his credibility as a medieval character but also providing the author with a foil for casting the desired light upon a given narrative situation. He warns, summarizes, comments, and forecasts, sometimes in verse.

Through the figure of Gaspard and the occasional reminders, in the text, that a first-person narrator is telling a story of which only he himself has knowledge, Storm achieves a degree of realism that establishes a much closer link between himself and the reader than does his usual technique of using a system of frames and lyrical passages. The reader's attention is thus directed upon events which must have a profound meaning, for otherwise they would not be worth telling. Instead of feeling the need to justify continually his imagined reality by simulating objective facts and motives, the narrator indicates his presence by brief remarks, such as "everything turned out differently"; "through all peril, love found a way"; "the raven had cawed; a breath of the weather to come may have touched it; from where it was to come it did not know. But I will tell you now." [81] Even through the similes the narrator remains visible as the commentator and omniscient source of the events: "but he [Rolf Lembeck] felt as if he feared the strong arms of his wife and proceeded down the path [from a rendezvous with Dagmar] as if into a valley of death." [82]

Like the narrative point of view, the symbols in the story serve to anticipate and amplify a situation. The artificial butterfly which was suspended from the poplar tree and which—when they were children—Dagmar's brother would shoot down, stands for Dagmar herself and for her happiness. When the Italian poplar ("a rarity in these parts," states the narrator—just as Dagmar and Rolf, we would add) is cut down Dagmar feels that her world has come to an end. Rolf, wearing the family crest of a hawk on his shirt, descends from the poplar like a bird of prey to meet his beloved, and he flings himself from the tower like a bird. Finally the messenger from Haderslevhuus, who appears dressed in the traditional and colorful attire of a wedding herald, is a toothless old man actually symbolizing death, the true content of his message.

A theme quite different from this novella is treated in two novellas which Storm had published under the title *With the Lower Classes* (*Bei kleinen Leuten*). Because of its structural properties and its theme one of these novellas shall be discussed.

VII A Doppelgänger

This novella, published in 1886 in six installments, had been commissioned by its publisher, Emil Franzos. The working-class figures of the cooper Basch and the laborer John Hansen, alias Glückstadt, are two portraits of members of the lower classes and represent a humanitarian point of view, or, as Storm wrote to his publisher, "I was well aware that both novellas, this one and its tandem part 'Bötjer Basch' exhibit the gospel of love." [83] Since the cooper's rescue from attempted suicide through the collective kindness of his fellow townsmen and the hounding and persecution of the social outcast John Hansen represent two aspects of the same theme, Storm had both novellas published in book form under a collective title in 1887.

The title of this novella alluding to the Romantic *Doppelgänger* motif, merely signifies the two sides of the same person: the unhappy life of the criminal John Glückstadt and the life of John Hansen, devoted father and husband. The story's opening part is told from the viewpoint of a first-person narrator who introduces himself as a lawyer and poet having stopped over for a time in an unidentified German town on a holiday trip. There he meets a middle-aged man, a forester, whose attention he attracts because of his Low German accent. He tells the narrator that his wife hails from the same region and invites him to stay at their home for a few days. During their conversation it develops that the forester's wife comes from the same town as the narrator and author and that her father's name was John Hansen. Later, during a stroll in the garden, the forester reveals the other name of her father, and the narrator is sworn to secrecy, since the woman does not know about the second identity of her father. At this point, the narrative rather abruptly changes to John Glückstadt's story, as the narrator gradually retrieves the "facts" from memory.

John Hansen, the son of a farmer, was without work after his discharge from the army. The town where he seeks to settle down remains unnamed, except for certain street names and other landmarks which would identify it as Husum. John's companion, an ex-convict by the name of Wenzel, talks him into committing a crime, skillfully exploiting the young man's sense of frustration and his longing for action. Appealing to his sense of sportsmanship, the two agree to burglarize the house of a prominent citizen in the town. The golden watch, John Hansen's share, turns up later in the possession of a relative to whom John had given it as a present. The object eventually leads to John's and Wenzel's arrest and conviction. John Hansen is sent to prison for six years in a town named Glückstadt. After his release he becomes known as John Glückstadt.

Because of the sympathy of some well-meaning townspeople the former convict obtains work on a nearby farm as the supervisor of the women laborers there. Eventually, he marries one of the young women, and they set up a household in her mother's tiny house on the edge of town. As time goes by, a child is born and a measure of happiness comes into their lives. John Glückstadt's past, however, does not permit them to plan their future in any meaningful way. After the sudden death of his employer, John is again without work. Poverty, hunger, and frustration build up to unbearable tension in their small abode. The couple begins to fight, and John is driven to laying a hand on his wife. After the mother's death, the small family lives in peace and harmony again with both Hanna and John working at odd jobs. John Glückstadt is discouraged and despairs over his inability to regain his honor as a man and citizen. By an unspoken agreement, his past is never mentioned in their home. During a quarrel one day, however, Hanna feels provoked beyond endurance and openly alludes to his criminal past. Beside himself, John pushes his wife away from him and she is flung against an iron stove. She is killed by a set-screw protruding from it. Their neighbor, a carpenter, is persuaded that it was an accident, and, with his cooperation, the manslaughter remains a secret.

John and Christine, his three-year-old daughter, go on living in abject poverty. John has made an arrangement with an old woman to live with them and to look after Christine. Because of his good relationship with the mayor of the town and his efforts to lead an honest life, he is seldom without work. One day, however, he is stopped by Wenzel on his way home from work. Wenzel had just been released from prison for another crime. A policeman who had stopped Wenzel to check his papers immediately spreads all over town that John and Wenzel had been conspiring to commit another crime. From now on, John is unable to find further employment in town. Christine, who is seven years old at this point, offers to go begging for food. As a last vestige of his pride, John refuses to have his daughter beg for him. Rather, on the same night he resolves to steal some potatoes from a nearby field where he had once worked as a supervisor. On that field is an abandoned well which was covered with rotten boards and into which he used to throw pebbles to see how deep it was. Eventually, he had his employer fence it in for everyone's safety. Now John is back for the second time as an act of desperation. In the previous winter when he had no money for fuel, he had come to steal the fence for firewood. Now, in search of potatoes at night he stumbles into the well and is killed. He is never found, and no one knows where to look for him or his body. Christine is adopted by the parents of the forester, and the narrator comes to recognize in her the little girl whose father was known to the whole town as the former criminal John Glückstadt.

At this point, the characters of the opening frame reappear, and the narrator tells the whole story to the forester who, in turn, resolves to tell his wife about the other side of John Hansen. She, who had remembered darkly her father's terrible outbursts of temper but consciously only his gentle concern for her after her mother's death, is now grateful to have these two images joined into that of "a whole human being."

As one contemporary critic wrote about Storm's novella, "the entire misery of 1887 and 1888 confronts us starkly through this contemporary portrait, executed with classical mastery." [84] The critic, Johannes Wedde, a Social Democrat, concludes that Storm sought to reconcile, or even resolve, the problem by having John's daughter live a normal and happy life with her husband and son. This is to symbolize that the gap between the poor and the middle class is to be bridged and that the majority of the German people are to partake of the enjoyment of a pure and full humanity. It is perhaps not difficult to interpret the meaning of *Ein Doppelgänger* in this way. Yet there are structural and stylistic indications which would render this interpretation a great deal less plausible.

The novella belongs to the already familiar type of the author functioning as a temporary first-person narrator in the frame as well as in the actual story. But this time Theodor Storm appears practically undisguised as a "lawyer and poet" in the frame. For this reason as well as certain references in the story proper, it is not difficult to identify the locale of the narrative as Husum on the North Sea. Thus the unusual social theme of this novella assumes a very personal significance. For example, the forester in the roadside tavern talks to him, because of the narrator's accent. When this becomes clear to him, he muses "so that's it! Do the native sounds reach so deep and are they therefore so indestructible?" [85] This is, as we have seen, a bedrock truth in Storm's whole being. He clings to this one certainty of homeland as if it were the only orientation in an otherwise chaotic universe. From there, Storm proceeds to retrieve his story in the familiar way of his chronicle novellas. From the vague "familiar sounds of home" to the revelation of John Glückstadt's identity, the author and narrator gradually remembers and reconstructs the story. The motivation given here is the fact that Glückstadt's fate was common knowledge in his native town. Thus the reminiscing narrator remains visible throughout the internal narrative, rather scrupulously separating the known facts from his additions or conjectures. The narrator, therefore, is forced constantly to set off report from speculation, such as the remark "no one saw it; yet after their deaths [John's and Hanna's] everyone talked about it." [86] The one structural feature, however, which comes unexpectedly is the report by the narrator that he had been in a semi-visionary state while recounting the plot of John Glückstadt's tale:

Gradually I became aware that I was far away from my hometown, standing by the open window in the house of the forester. . . . I checked my watch: it was after one o'clock! The candle on the table had almost burned down. In a semi-visionary state—something I had been prone to since my youth—I had seen passing before my eyes a whole lifetime of a human being whose end, at the time it occurred, had remained a mystery to me as well. Now, suddenly, I knew. . . .[87]

This surprising admission lends a different flavor to the story itself and to its conclusion in the frame. The story's raison d'être was to shed light on John Hansen's full identity. His daughter, the forester's wife, knows of the two irreconcilable sides of her father's life and is troubled by it. The narrator's motive for telling the tale is to fuse the two contradictory images present in Christine's mind into a whole. This humanitarian impulse—the very concrete reason for telling the story in the first place—conflicts with the narrator's trancelike state,[88] because it could be argued that the real role of the narrator was to make the vision the object of interest. The semi-conscious state of the narrator actually borders closely on the interior-monologue technique of the Impressionists. Taken by itself, the vision concerns an individual tragic fate the knowledge and transmission of which is quite accidental. Inevitably, the depiction of this human tragedy had to take precedence over the novella's implicit social criticism.

In this connection it is of interest that Storm had originally intended to call the novella "The Well" (Der Brunnen). Neither the discarded title, nor the present one give any indication that the theme of social discrimination, crime, and poverty was the raison d'être of the novella. The central role of the well in the story makes it a motif in the same way as the idea of the dual personality of the main character, the loss of his honor, his fist, and the loss of happiness are important motifs in the narrative. From this list of motifs, to say nothing of the title and the vision, it is clear where the emphasis in this novella is to be put. There are several comments by the narrator which express his opinion about the plight of Glückstadt's social class. They and the four main motifs, however, always stress the personal nature of this individual fate. In this way, almost imperceptibly, Storm lends more weight to the personal plight of this human being than upon the reasons for this plight and a possible solution. It is the temper and emotional state of John Glückstadt which guide his hand rather than his power of reasoning. He is the victim of circumstances. It is their lack of education which victimizes the members of Glückstadt's social class, as the narrator emphasizes repeatedly. He also remarks with some condescension that "most of these people—not a bad sort, actually—live their lives and have their eyes trained upon today and tomorrow; what has been and what is past does not teach them anything." [89]

The motif of the well which is also a symbol, however, moves the story into close proximity to the chronicle novellas as far as their tragic core is concerned. The only difference is that the well, as an object and remnant of the past, is introduced at the end of the novella, because it is precisely its mystery—the mystery of John Hansen's death—which caused the narrator to reconstruct or rescue his story to begin with, very much like the fading manuscript or the ruin of a structure in the author's native region which prompts him to preserve its story for posterity. Thus the narrator in the concluding frame tells the reader that he can now recall the report of a young boy who, on the morning after John Glückstadt's disappearance, was passing the well while catching butterflies and had heard an eery cry issuing from its depth calling out the name of Christine. Thus the narrator purports to be certain of Glückstadt's place of death.

John Glückstadt's life was one of guilt and martyrdom. It is, as the mayor says at the end of the story, "after this John had atoned for his guilt according to the law he was, as is customary, turned over to his dear fellow man to be hounded. And he has been hounded to death by him, for he is without mercy. What is there to say? If I am to express an opinion, you should leave him be, for he now belongs to a different judge." [90] It is the tragedy of his death, the tragedy of man's mortality, however, that is more important than the reasons for his martyrdom. The symbol of the well, standing for a dark, mysterious fate, becomes the universal sign of mortality and lost happiness. It was by the well that John met Hanna for the first time and "happiness dwelt among the couple." Later, it was the wooden fence around it which saved John and his daughter from freezing to death on an icy Christmas Eve. The accidental killing of Hanna marks the final turning point in his life and the disappearance of happiness from it. The well has now become the receptacle of John's hopes and happiness. He tells Christine of her mother's death, "we didn't think of death! . . . but it is always with us; just beckon with your finger and it will come!" [91] Thus, the well assumes symbolic meaning for Glückstadt's happiness as well as for his death. The tragic meaning of this novella lies in the fact that man can be the victim of his fellow man just as he is limited by the forces of nature which Storm never tired of portraying in his stories. The ultimate tragedy finds its pathetic expression in the mayor's words that John Glückstadt now belongs to a different judge.

One year after the publication of this somewhat flawed work, Theodor Storm was to write his masterpiece and, in many ways, the artistic solution to his lifelong struggle with the desperate problem of the meaning of life in a meaningless reality.

VIII   *The Rider on the White Horse*

Der Schimmelreiter appeared in 1888, a few weeks before the author's death. It is his most impressive achievement. In both structure and language the novella marks a high point in German literature of the second half of the century. The story is based upon a dike legend which Storm had read in his youth. The first reference to it is found in a letter to Theodor Mommsen, dating from 1843.[92] The subject preoccupied Storm throughout his life until it came to fruition shortly before his death. The novella is his longest; however, it is not merely its length but also its concentration on the development of the hero and the events which ensue (rather than the concentration upon a central event, so typical of the novella) that would justify the term "character novel" to define this narrative.

In 1886 Storm wrote to Heyse: "Further on the drawing board: 'Der Schimmelreiter,' a dike story; a hard nut to crack, because it means to rest the legend of a dike-ghost on the four legs of a novella without obscuring its uncanny character." [93] Storm achieves this blending of legend and reality by employing a triple frame involving three different narrators. The "novel" thus represents an optimum of objectivity, because it succeeds in integrating the author, that is, the first-person narrator, in the narrative without sacrificing the objective attitude of the two narrators of the second and third frames.

In the opening paragraph or first frame, the author-narrator introduces himself as follows:

What I intend to report I learned more than half a century ago in the house of my great-grandmother, the widow of Senator Feddersen, while I, sitting by her easy chair, was busy reading a magazine bound in blue cardboard; I cannot recall whether it was the "Leipziger" or "Pappes Hamburger Lesefrüchte." I still feel it like a shiver running through me as, in the process, the gentle hand of the octogenarian from time to time tenderly stroked the hair of her great-grandson. She herself and that distant time have long since ceased to exist; since then, I have also tried in vain to locate those pages, and therefore, I cannot vouch for the veracity of the facts, much less rise to defend them if someone wanted to challenge them. I can only state unequivocally that I have never forgotten them, although they were not brought back to the surface for any external reason.[94]

From this point on, the second narrator, the first-person reporter of the magazine story, picks up the thread. He tells how, during a storm, he rode along a dike in northern Frisia. We infer from the time reference made by the author-narrator of the opening frame that this must have happened around the year 1830. It is on this ride that the first reference to the rider on the white horse is made. "Now, however, something approached me on the dike; I heard nothing; but more and more clearly I thought I could make out a dark figure whenever the half moon shed its dim light upon it; and soon, as it came nearer, I could see it; it was sitting on a horse, a long-legged emaciated white horse; a dark cloak was billowing about its shoulders and, in passing, two burning eyes stared at me from a pale face." [95] The narrator goes on to describe what he saw, namely that the phantom seemed to have disappeared in a breach which a storm had opened in the dike. When he arrives at an inn nearby, the people there whom he tells what he has seen reply almost in fear that he had seen the "Schimmelreiter." The dikegrave and his deputies are present to await the outcome of the storm and to supervise any repairs which may become necessary. The dikegrave assures the narrator that the appearance of the rider need not mean a disaster for everyone here, because "in '17 it struck our neighbors over there; may they be prepared for anything!"⁹⁶ At this point, the schoolmaster of the village, a short, hunchbacked, and sickly old man interrupts the dikegrave to tell the narrator what he knows about the ghost rider. The dikegrave warns the narrator of the schoolmaster's arrogance, because once in his youth he had studied theology, and therefore he would not tell the story the way his old housekeeper, Antje Vollmers, has always told it. The schoolmaster dismisses such talk and apologizes for the superstitious aspects of his tale in advance. The narrator assures him that he was quite capable of "separating the wheat from the chaff."

The schoolmaster now proceeds to tell the story in objective third-person mode. In the middle of the eighteenth century, the well-read Tede Haien lived here. Already in his youth his son Hauke maintained that the dike's construction was faulty. Hauke is described as intelligent and as having inherited a mathematical talent because "Frisians are excellent reckoners." Soon Hauke enters the service of Tede Volkerts, the dikegrave, as a handyman. He is able to make many suggestions for the improvement of the dike on the basis of his calculations. It is no secret in the village that Tede Volkerts was made dikegrave because of his wealth, and not for his intelligence. More and more, Tede Volkerts comes to rely upon Hauke's help to keep the books in order and straighten out the accounts. Hauke's quiet rival is the foreman Ole Peters who envies him his position of trust with the dikegrave. Elke, the dikegrave's daughter, and Hauke soon become very attached to each other. When Ole Peters marries, he leaves the dikegrave's service and Hauke Haien becomes foreman. But he soon has to quit his post in order to tend his sick father. After the latter's death, however, he manages to help Tede Volkerts with his bookkeeping.

At this point in the narrative, the schoolmaster is interrupted by a messenger returning from the dike who exclaims: "The white horse rider has plunged into the breach!"⁹⁷ Whereupon the dikegrave and his helpers leave the inn to check the mere in the dike. The narrator and the schoolmaster retire to the latter's room where he resumes his narration.

Hauke's and Elke's wish is that he become dikegrave. The only serious obstacle in his way is the fact that Hauke does not own enough land to satisfy an important prerequisite for the position. Hauke is also contemptuous of his rival's claims to the position, although he begins to fear him too, because he had recently inherited more land than Hauke possessed. Elke, however, counsels patience, as the obvious solution would be their marriage as a fulfillment of their deep love and affection and as a practical step toward achieving Hauke's ambition. Shortly afterward, Tede Volkerts dies. When the head-dikegrave begins to search for his successor, Elke succeeds in convincing him that Hauke would be the right man. Hauke is soon appointed and he and Elke are married, the precondition of Hauke's appointment. Hauke is dedicated to his office. He begins to draw up plans for a new outer dike, in order to turn the mud-flats behind it into a permanent polder which would yield pastures and fertile land for the community. After lengthy negotiations, his project is approved by the head-dikegrave. On the same day Hauke acquires from a "swarthy Slovac" on his way home, a haggard, undernourished young white horse. The purchase was a bargain. Through patient care, the horse soon regains its strength and turns into a lively and healthy animal which tolerates only its master on its back. Hauke's men live in superstitious fear of the animal, and a rumor spreads that the horse had risen from the skeleton of a horse which used to bleach in the sun on a sandbar off the coast, for since the purchase of the white horse by Hauke, the skeleton has disappeared from the sandbar.

The dikegrave now proceeds to settle the details of the construction of his new dike. He has to struggle against the prejudice of the villagers, who are opposed to innovation and resent his efficiency and superiority. Hauke drives himself and the others hard during the summer months, but he does not succeed in finishing the new dike before the onset of winter. All this happens nine years after Hauke and Elke are married and he is made dikegrave. That winter, Hauke and Elke are to become parents. The little girl, Wienke, is born feeble-minded, a cruel and ironic blow to this intelligent couple. In the next year the new dike is completed.

In the following years, Hauke continues to administer his office conscientiously, but he continues to have difficulties with the villagers in having repairs carried out. After an illness and in a weakened state of mind, he permits himself to be persuaded by his old rival and deputy Ole Peters to undertake minimal repairs on the old dike which had sustained some extensive but well-concealed damage in a recent storm. This moment of weakness is to have dire consequences for all. During a severe tidal wave, Hauke discovers a breach in the dike where he should have insisted upon much more extensive repairs. His wife and child whom he believes safely in the house, situated on a rise, have gone out in the storm to look for him. He can see them driving toward the dike but cannot stop them. The wind drowns out his voice. The waters that are rushing through the gap in the old dike carry them away. In despair and as if to give in to the superstitious villagers, who claim that only a living being thrown into the breach can restore it, he shouts "Oh God, take me; spare the others!" He then forces his horse into the waves, where both perish. The schoolmaster concludes his narration by saying that, since that time, the villagers claim to have seen the skeleton on the sandbar again. The storm outside has stopped in the meantime and on the next morning the narrator rides to town down the Hauke Haien Dike which still stands, a hundred years after it was built.

Storm wished to strike a balance between the legendary character of the story and its realistic setting. Perhaps it is fair to say that its basic technique lies in its deliberate ambiguity. Without committing himself, the author presents reason and irrationality, intelligence and ignorance, enlightenment and superstition in constant juxtaposition. This principle determines the structure of the novella. The triple frame is not only "a proper setting for such a rich painting inside, i.e., setting the proper distance, except for the first frame to which the author does not return," [98] but it is also an integral part of the story's structure. Thus, the author-narrator of the opening frame emphasizes that he cannot recall the source for his story and vouch for its accuracy. By this means he contrives to give its contents a greater degree of probability than if he had insisted on the truth of it. A similar effect is achieved by the other two narrators. The schoolmaster who narrates the main part of the story reports in the third person, therefore purporting to report fact rather than fiction. "Since the magazine narrator assumes only the role of an intermediary, his narrative about the phantom rider has the effect of a realistic event. The uncanny apparition is, therefore, introduced as something entirely probable. The validity of this phenomenon is soon underscored by the reaction of the group at the inn to the report of the messenger: "an expression of horror" emanates from it. For all of them the white horse rider obviously has "a concrete meaning." [99]

This technique represents a maximum degree of objectivity for Storm, whereby he succeeds in integrating myth and reality to make visible at least a potential transcendence through the tragedy of Hauke Haien, or in Storm's own words—by way of a progress report to Heyse: "on page 92 Hauke Haien, the boy, has become a dikegrave; now artistic skill is needed to transform the dikegrave into a phantom." [100]

The balance achieved in the narrative is one of giving equal space to the superstitious fears and ignorance of the villagers and to Hauke Haien's intelligence and his high level of consciousness. Moreover, the rationalistic schoolmaster with his modern skepticism is starkly contrasted with the uncanny subject of his tale. Also, as Walter Silz points out, the schoolmaster's attitude toward his story must be taken with a grain of salt, because he has an ax to grind. He is described as a sickly and deformed man who is critical of society and his mental inferiors and loves to champion the representative of the enlightenment in Hauke. This sheds the proper light upon his statement in the closing frame to the effect that Hauke Haien was a spiritual leader like Socrates and Christ whom humanity has "ever crucified and burned." [101] Both enlightened figures, Hauke and the schoolmaster, are not only set off against the supernatural aspects of the story, but they are also linked with them.

The phantom of the White Horse Rider appears three times in the story. Each time, it is acknowledged as a real occurrence by its observers. Immediately preceding its second sighting, even the schoolmaster is moved to remark, " 'God knows!' . . . "there are things on this earth which can confuse the heart of an honest Christian;' " [102] This transformation of the realistic hero into a supernatural phenomenon has been criticized as contradicting the dispassionate viewpoint adopted toward these elements of the story.[103] It is our contention, however, that this is the novella's real aim: to create the myth of a modern tragic hero whose legend—his monument, the dike—survives and whose tragedy stands as a meaningful sign in a quasi-Faustian sense.[104] It is not, of course, the Goethean promise of a metaphysical redemption but a tentative solution in the way of a transcendental potential. The myth has become reality; it is believed by the people, by posterity. Hauke's myth has produced a positive result. Although the people at the inn are frightened, they are also secure in the knowledge that the dike has stood for a hundred years and that it will hold in the future, because the storm which was raging while Hauke Haien's legend was recounted had done only minor damage to the dike.[105]

The three apparitions are an integral part of the narrative, because from the moment of Hauke's purchase of the white horse, Hauke is closely linked with the supernatural, and "while yet alive he assumes the lineaments of legend (e.g., his haggard face, flashing eyes, and the fiery horse as a recurring motif to describe his appearance)." [106] Similarly, Hauke's report to his wife Elke about the circumstances of the purchase shows a trace of wonderment about the whole affair:

And then, woman, I shook the fellow's brown hand which he extended to me and which almost looked like a claw. And so we've got the white horse and for a song, I think. But it was certainly strange how, when I rode away, I heard laughter behind me, and as I turned my head, I saw the Slovak; he was still standing there, legs apart, arms crossed behind his back and laughing at me like the devil.[107]

By the same token, rider and horse become as one, and the white horse tolerates no other rider. The horse seems to develop its own will, as the frequent references to it indicate: "and the horse pushed forward," "no sooner had he mounted than the animal whinnied as with extreme delight; and it flew off with him, down the hill and toward the dike. . . ." Finally, as Walter Silz points out, it is, ironically, the clear-headed Hauke who throws himself into the breach in the dike, thereby closing it forever, while during the dike repairs earlier, he was the one who prevented the immuring of a dog in the dike by the superstitious laborers.[108]

Just as there is a bipolar structure of the story as a whole, so is there a notable dialectic of the motif of death as collective and individual tragedy, that is, as a deterministic and an ethical problem.

In the double unity of rider and horse and of horse and natural phenomena two things seem to converge: for one thing, the emotional disposition of the dikegrave through the unity of rider and horse, and the force of events to which Hauke is increasingly subjected by the near finality of the horse's activity (its almost independent action which seems to anticipate its master's will). Through the unity of rider and horse, and of the horse with the forces of nature, the events assume the character of inevitability, i.e., one which raises them above the level of a purely subjective flaw in the dikegrave—on the basis of a personal fault which Hauke acknowledges at the end—to the level of a reality experienced as absolute and from which the Self cannot escape. Tragedy here is not a unique and avoidable catastrophe but represents an inescapable condition of life. . . . Tragedy [depends on] the character's perspective upon life or reality . . . herein lie the conditions of life for Hauke.[109]

The deterministic character of Storm's concept of tragedy and tragic guilt has already been discussed. In addition, the familiar death motif ought to be mentioned. It threads through *Der Schimmelreiter* just as consistently as it does through most of Storm's other works. Nature, for example, appears as a pernicious force, its symbol being the sea. Thus, on the morning after the storm and the family's death, nature shows a face of serene calm as the narrator rides back to town "in the most brilliant sunshine which had risen over a scene of vast destruction." The rather extensive description of Tede Volkert's funeral, occurring about midway in the narratvie, introduces the death motif by way of a Low German proverb inscribed on the grave stone of the family grave: "This is death which devours everything, / Science and the Arts, / The brilliant man has now departed, / May God grant him blessed resurrection." Above the inscription there is a skull with a prominent set of teeth.[110] Its central location in the story makes this motif one of prefiguring not only Hauke's death but the death of all men. The horse's skeleton, which reappears on the sandbar after the hero's tragic end, is another reminder of man's mortality. The new dike stands symbolically between life and death and provides a dramatic unity of place and action as well as a line between darkness and enlightenment (the hostility of the villagers and specifically of their leader, Hauke's rival Ole Peters and Hauke's superior intelligence) and between man and natural disaster. It is also the battle line between the natural and the supernatural, a fluid front, because the sea gnaws at the dike and man's defenses are broken down.[111]

The individual side of the tragedy, on the other hand, constitutes no less a part of the whole than its deterministic elements. The ethical, personal guilt of the hero is stated in classic Aeschylean terms, incorporating the three major elements which constitute tragedy: the inevitable course of the tragic events, the tragic consciousness of the hero, and his tragic guilt. Just as with Aeschylus, Hauke Haien is guilty of hubris, the overweening pride which violates the natural order of things, although only in a moral and ethical sense, since there is no metaphysical concept to be found in Theodor Storm similar to the universal mythology of classical antiquity or to the *ordo mundi* of the Christian Middle Ages. Thus, when Hauke feels how he is being opposed in his rightful ambition to succeed the old dikegrave Tede Volkerts, he has visions of hostile faces and is gripped by anger toward these people, "for they wanted to keep him from the one office for which of all men only he had a calling.—And he could not banish these thoughts; they kept returning, and so, in his young heart, there was growing not only integrity and love but also hatred and pride." [112] After his appointment, Hauke is also stung by the accusation that he has become dikegrave only because of his wife, and he vows to earn the title through his own accomplishments. In a moment of excessive pride (brought on by the discovery that the people have quite naturally taken to calling the new polder after its architect rather than by its official designation), Hauke Haien repeats to himself the words he has just heard: "Hauke Haien Polder! Hauke Haien Polder! In his mind the new dike almost turned into the eighth wonder of the world; there was nothing like it in all of Frisia! . . . he felt as if he were standing in the midst of all Frisians; he was towering above them all, and his eyes lit on them with keenness and pity." [113] Finally, in a moment of physical weakness and after years of mental strain, he permits himself to be persuaded by shoddy arguments and agrees to only superficial repairs of the old dike which is badly damaged below the watermark; this he does mainly for the sake of peace and good will on the part of his deputy and the villagers. It is this fatal flaw which augurs disaster and which, together with his hubris, proves Hauke's undoing. When disaster strikes and the dike breaks to flood the new polder, Hauke is aware of his sin of omission of the previous summer: "O Lord, I confess, . . . I have tended my office badly!," for, as he well knew, nobody but he himself had recognized the weakness in the old dike, and he should have insisted on the proper course of action.[114]

Hauke's death, finally, is more than merely an act of despair. It is an act of self-sacrifice for the sake of his life's work (perhaps as an unconscious admission to the myth-giving powers of the people who also believe that only a living being can secure the last section of the dike)—to assure his legend—as well as an act of atonement commensurate with his mission, accomplishments, and guilt. The conflicting aspects of his character, the love for his family, his personal integrity, and his arrogance and moment of fatal weakness are also reconciled by his death. In this way, it means more than just the material extinction so prevalent in Storm's other novellas.

But there is yet another side to Hauke's character. We have already alluded to it in our discussion of the Stormian novellas in general. It concerns the monumental side of this literary figure, not unlike Nietzsche's superman and C. F. Meyer's Thomas Becket (*The Saint—Der Heilige*), to name two examples. Thus Hauke Haien has been called a figure typical of the imperialistic age of Bismarck, at least to the extent he differs from the historical context of the Age of Enlightenment, namely through his portrayal in a heroic light, typical of Storm's own time.[115] The new myth exemplified by this tragic hero, although eclectic in an imperialistic age, is seen against a dull, insolent mass. All of that is cast into even greater relief by Storm's technique of creating a "noble distance" from his material by introducing three frames around the story proper. From the hero emerges a basic contrast between bourgeois ethics and the right of the genius to assert himself and to defy normal rules of behavior. These forces are in constant confrontation in the form of an ideal and its criticism, that is, the moral evaluation of the "superman." Thus, in the end, the dike remains, although the hero must perish. Walter Silz points to a brief passage in the novella which epitomizes the aspect of monumentality in Hauke: "At the zenith of his success, we . . . see him in statuesque and symbolic pose, on his dike, dominating for a space these two enemies: the storm-whipped sea on one side and reluctant men, bending to his iron will, on the other" (K.VII, 341).[116]

The tragic hero, then, is Storm's tentative answer to the vicissitudes of the materialistic nihilism of his own age. He involves himself as the author-narrator in the opening frame to indicate, subconsciously perhaps, the importance he attaches to the events portrayed in the story. The careful balance of the various contrasting structural elements of the novella (also the balance or parallelism between narrative and narrated time, that is, the time or space the narrator expends on a given phase or time span of the narrative proper) tends to focus the attention ever more sharply upon the hero and the intense drama that accompanies the fateful phases of his life (at the end of his life, Hauke is roughly forty years old). Hauke's tragedy is profoundly moving not only because of his personal guilt but also because it is presented with the detachment that characterizes the entire piece, the author's brief intrusion (perhaps unnecessarily) notwithstanding. The author's commitment lies in his search for a redemptive force which he sees in the redeeming potential of reason and myth. The promise which Hauke's tragic death holds for mankind lies in the dike, the enduring monument to his ceaseless efforts, and the legend to which his extraordinary life has given rise. Within the limits of his entire oeuvre, the fully contoured hero who is the cause of the events depicted in the story, who is held accountable for his actions, and who is at once real and mythical, makes this novella Storm's crowning achievement. It concerns the very difficult but at the same time noble subject of the human spirit and the human potential. For this reason alone it ranks with the best literature of Storm's own country and time.

CHAPTER 5

A Summary: Storm's Significance as a Writer and Poet Today

IF the favorable reception of an artist on the part of his countrymen and foreign audiences is any index of his worth, Theodor
Storm has not fared too badly. His works continue to appear in
new editions intended for a large audience in both Germanies,
and many of his books and poems have been translated into several European languages as well as into Chinese and Japanese.[1]
On the other hand, only esthetic criteria can be applied to the
question of an artist's significance with any degree of accuracy.

As a representative of that group of nineteenth-century writers
commonly referred to as "realists," Storm shared in their regional-
ism and the basic human concerns expressed in their writings. As
we have seen from the analysis of *Hans und Heinz Kirch*, he was,
in many ways, a forerunner of Impressionism in his subjectivity
and the prominence of the motifs of transiency and death in his
works. Storm's contemporary Fontane, whose novel *Effie Briest,*
for example, represents an even stronger prefiguration of the Im-
pressionist school (by the occurrences of interior monologue, for
instance), was keenly aware of Storm's subjectivity which he felt
to be typically "Stormian." In his essay on Storm, written in 1853,
he emphasized the latter's "poetic soul," his "sensibility," and
"depth and inwardness," and yet—or, perhaps, because of it—
counted him among the realists. Fontane saw quite clearly that
Storm could gain access to reality only via the expression of subjective experience.[2]

In 1889, one year after Storm's death, Fontane remarked in response to a questionnaire asking him to list the "best books"
known to him and those which had had a particular significance
for him as a writer, "I like everything by Storm, especially his
poems; they are equal to the best we have. Entirely a parallel to
Mörike but more significant in their totality." [3]

Storm's peculiarity as a writer and a man, as I have attempted to sketch it in these pages, would appear to be great artistic integrity and patient craftsmanship. Between *Immensee* and *Der Schimmelreiter* stretches a lifetime of struggle to overcome a deep-seated pessimism, and his last novella reflects in part, at least, Storm's conquest of this attitude. The intensity of the private experience, the inwardness of his nature may have prevented him from attaining an ironic attitude toward life. He was no thinker, but he had a well-developed sense of language and style: his craft[4] was designed to stress intensity and immediacy in simple, almost conventional images whose power lay in their rhythmic and emotional elements. To be sure, the pathetic gesture prevails over the tragic in his works. His deterministic and mechanistic concept of tragedy (for a long time he rejected personal guilt as too legalistic) and the allegorization of the truth—claiming general application of limited individual experience portrayed in his work—make Theodor Storm an epigone, an eclectic.[5] This, of course, was not only a personal failing but also a condition of a generation of writers in Germany, Switzerland, and Austria who wrote in a period of cultural and political transition and mediocrity, that is, between the styles of the *Biedermeier* or restoration period and of Naturalism and Impressionism.

If one were to assess Storm's place in the history of European literature of his own time, he as well as numerous other contemporaries of similar stature—C. F. Meyer, Gottfried Keller, Adalbert Stifter, Jeremias Gotthelf, Wilhelm Raabe, to name a few—would not come off very well, the yardstick being the great issues of the time and their literary treatment. This has been done repeatedly by pointing to the backwardness of the social and political scene in Germany, most notably by Erich Auerbach, Georg Lukács, and Robert Minder.[5] Storm never has been and never will be considered of a stature equal to that of Tolstoi, Dostoevsky, or Balzac, for example. On the other hand, Wolfgang Preisendanz in his recent Storm essay, quoting Vladimir Nabokov, reminds us that "only its art, never its social significance, can protect a work of the imagination from larvae and rust," and Preisendanz goes on to say that if this were not the case it would be a mystery why a work of fiction can be more than merely a literary, a cultural, or a social document, and it would remain incomprehensible why Flaubert became a classic novelist and Gutzkow did not.[6]

At its best, it is Storm's relentless artistic struggle depicting

the human condition, the transitoriness of all things, which continues to account for his deserved durability, though his style may
range from the sentimental at its worst to the genuinely tragic at
its most sublime. He worked on the language of his poetry and of
his prose as ruthlessly as any artist has ever done who had a vision
of how it ought to be.

Notes and References

Preface

A summary of the theoretical views described in Richard Brinkmann, *Wirklichkeit und Illusion. Studien über Gehalt und Grenzen des Begriffes Realismus für die erzählende Dichtung des 19. Jahrhunderts.* Tübingen: Max Niemeyer, 1957.

Brinkmann seeks to arrive at a more conclusive definition of the term "literary realism" than heretofore held by literary scholarship. He questions the validity of the assumption that realism in literature denotes the representation of external or empirical reality. Above all, Brinkmann expresses doubt in the methods through which the definition was arrived at, because the methodology involved merely extraneous criteria such as the authorship, history, style, and motifs of a literary work.

Instead, Brinkmann demonstrates that a work of literature must be regarded as an autonomous (nonhistorical) entity and that only by considering those criteria which are not accidental to a work but inherent in it can the proper constituent parts be derived for a definition of literary realism:

> Expressed in the language of school logic: the material object of the term realism (always meaning the realism of nineteenth-century literature) concerns the structural forms of literature, i.e., those forms through which literature constructs the world represented by it, as its own reality. Everything else derives its validity for a definition of literary realism from these forms and from a perspective determined by them. By the same token, this approach is indispensable if one wants to arrive at a term defining a literary period, representing more than merely a transposition from other areas of knowledge. . . . In this sense, the term "literary realism of the nineteenth century" has yet to be defined. (pp. 79–80)

As a philosophical basis for his investigation, Brinkmann quotes from a statement by the English physicist A. S. Eddington which points to the difficulties encountered in the search for factualness and objectivity:

> Actuality has been lost in the exigency of the chase . . . We have torn away the mental fancies to get at the reality beneath, only to find that the reality of that which is beneath is bound up with its potentiality of awakening these fancies. It is because the mind, the weaver of illusion, is also the only guarantor of reality that reality is always to be sought at the base of illusion. (p. 319)

Brinkmann proposes to interpret three novellas according to problems characteristic of nineteenth-century literature, that is, chiefly the writer's problem of coming to grips with reality as it really is. The three novellas demonstrate these problems and their effects in certain characteristic states of development. The three novellas are Grillparzer's *Der arme Spielmann,* Ludwig's *Zwischen Himmel und Erde,* and Keyserling's *Beate und Mareile.* Both Grillparzer and Ludwig attempted to isolate their characters' subjective experience in order to set it off from an "objective" view of reality. Grillparzer was at pains to separate these subjective and objective perspectives of his hero by introducing a narrator whose function is to be a wholly detached observer. Keyserling, however, advanced to the realization that subject and object can no longer be distinguished in fiction. He believed that reality exists only as subjective experience, although he still insisted upon setting off his characters' private experience from its objective observation, i.e., he separated internal events from extraneous reality.

The problem of nineteenth-century literature is the individual and his relationship to reality. As yet, the outstanding writers of the century (Brinkmann considers his three examples to be typical of a whole group) do not break radically with the trappings of a realistic style which is circumscribed by the exigencies of the logical categories of time and space. The dilemma arose, because these writers were intent upon preserving a meaningful totality or a total meaning of life. It was a struggle for tradition, for a Goethean idealism, and for a normative value of art which expressed itself chiefly in ethical terms. Man's relationship to an atomized, hence, arbitrary concept of reality was to be made total by superimposing an ethical nexus (as in the social novels by Fontane) or a historical nexus as in the historical novels of the century to provide a concept of continuity.

Gradually this normative residue disappears. Prose fiction now represents only the manner in which reality itself appears, or rather, how individuals experience and how they exist. This stage represents the optimal typological fulfillment in the development of realism. At this point, however, the fulfillment proves the original nature of realistic intent to be unattainable, which is indeed a dialectical reversal. Highest fulfillment is already the end and overcoming of its original nature. Because out of the original desire to represent objective reality emerges the very specific subjective reality of the individual if one removes all idealizing and normative additions. This development continues with a certain unreflected naïveté into the literary phases of naturalism and impressionism. Externally the form appears to be that of the objective representation of an objective reality. To be sure, the poets had been aware for some time of the relativity of their view of reality. According to Brinkmann, there is a certain skepticism that threads through the narratives of many of the realists, and this all the more so, the more decisively they forego the claim to any normative totality in their works. This is very much in evidence in the case of Theodor Fontane whose works derive their charm from this skepticism. Even Grillparzer and Keller show a tendency in this direction, although they had not yet consciously reduced reality to the experience of the subject. Their works are ahead of their consciousness. Even during the period of impressionism there existed narratives which represented a complete subjectification of reality in form and theme while retaining the semblance of a realistic mode of narration.

Brinkmann is careful to separate the old form of the first person narrative from the new type of monologue novella of impressionism. Schnitzler's *Leutnant Gustl* (1900) represents such a monologue novella in which an extremely uneventful reality exists only as a subjective reflection in the narrator. The traditional first person narrative, on the other hand, depicts events and experiences as real, although from the perspective of the narrator and as relating to his Self. Hence, despite the first person form, there still exists a duality of reality and experience, a distance between subject and object. Hence, it is exactly because of the first person style in which the narrator is tangible reality that subjective experience remains concretized as objective. In the monologue novella this is quite different. Here, we no longer have the distinction between the perspective upon reality and the personal experiences in the encounter with reality; for there is no longer a distance between the two, because in these interior monologue novellas plot has become immaterial. What the nineteenth century had understood to be reality, is now merely the point of departure for actual reality as it is seen now, i.e., experiences, insights of the character. The issue is not the subjective perspective in the experience of a real event, but the exciting experience of an experienced event within the subject itself, having its own dynamic properties and laws. This gives rise to a new experience of time which is separate from experienced time and —having become conscious—in turn produces new inward experiences. Thus, finally, reality as objective fact apart from the subject has been exploded as a superficial deception, as non-reality, as illusion. Nineteenth-century realism is at an end.

Chapter One
(For abbreviations see Preface)

1. "Erinnerungen an die Lübecker Gymnasiastenzeit und an Ferdinand Röse," K. VIII, 15.

2. "Aus der Jugendzeit," K. VIII, 3–7.

3. *Briefwechsel zwischen Theodor Storm und Eduard Mörike,* ed. Hanns Wolfgang Rath (Stuttgart, 1919), pp. 69–70.

4. K. VIII, 7.

5. Gertrud Storm, *Mein Vater Theodor Storm* (Berlin, 1922), p. 35.

6. K. I, 226.

7. *Briefwechsel zwischen Theodor Storm und Emil Kuh,* ed. Paul R. Kuh, *Westermanns Monatshefte,* II (1889–90), 272.

8. K. III, 155.

9. "Theodor Storm und Heinrich Seidel im Briefwechsel," ed. Wolfgang Seidel, *Deutsche Rundschau,* CLXXXVIII (1921), 201.

10. K. I, 243. This is the third of eight stanzas. For the entire poem, cf. Peter Goldammer, *Theodor Storm. Eine Einführung in Leben und Werk* (Leipzig, 1966), pp. 41–42.

11. Cf. Franz Stuckert, "Der handschriftliche Nachlass Storms und seine Bedeutung für die Forschung," *Schriften der Theodor-Storm-Gesellschaft,* I (1952), 41–60.

12. Franz Stuckert, *Theodor Storm. Sein Leben und seine Welt* (Bremen, 1955), p. 54.

13. *Nachgelassene Schriften,* ed. Gertrud Storm, vol. IV: *Briefe an seine Freunde* (Braunschweig, 1917).

14. *Adel des Geistes* (Stockholm, 1955), pp. 460 ff.

15. *Theodor Storm–Paul Heyse, Briefwechsel,* Clifford A. Bernd, ed. (Berlin, 1969), I, 95; 100 ff.

16. *Theodor Storms Briefwechsel mit Theodor Mommsen,* Erich Teitge, ed. (Weimar, 1966).

17. K. I, 122.

18. Peter Goldammer, *Theodor Storm, ibid.,* pp. 87–88.

19. Franz Stuckert, *op. cit.,* p. 83.

20. From an unpublished letter to his father-in-law Ernst Esmarch, June 18, 1865. Schleswig-Holsteinische Landesbibliothek.

21. The term is self-contradictory, given the dramatic character of the genre; by rather consistent usage, however, the designation chronicle novella for Storm's later works proves a convenient frame of reference.

22. K. I, 253.

23. Stuckert, *op. cit.,* p. 114.

Chapter Two

1. Juli 1886. *Briefe an Dorothea Jensen und Georg Westermann,* ed. Ewald Lüpke (Braunschweig, 1942).

2. Theodor Storm, *Sämtliche Werke,* ed. Peter Goldammer (Berlin, 1967), I, 7.

3. This copy is housed in the repository of the Schleswig-Holsteinische Landesbibliothek in Kiel, Germany.

4. Franz Stuckert, *Theodor Storm: Sein Leben und seine Welt* (Bremen, 1955), pp. 169 ff.

5. Cf. the interpretation of the poem by Walter Silz, "Theodor Storm: Three Poems," *Germanic Review,* 42 (1967), pp. 296 ff.

6. No date; cf. Stuckert, p. 188.

7. Dec. 10, 1852, in *Nachgelassene Schriften,* ed. Gertrud Storm, IV: *Briefe an seine Freunde* (Braunschweig, 1917).

8. Cf. the poems "O bleibe treu den Toten" und "Es ist ein Flüstern," where the subject seeks rapport with the dead beyond any physical reality.

9. Cf. Clifford Bernd, *Theodor Storm's Craft of Fiction: The Torment of a Narrator* (Chapel Hill, 1966). The torment here refers to the conflict between transiency and reminiscence. "The narrator of Theodor Storm's prose fiction is a tormented intelligence ever oscillating between two conflicting thoughts . . . the . . . maw of passing time . . . and . . . his ability to overcome his phobia . . . ," p. 7.

10. G. I, 110.

11. Cf. the interpretation of "Abseits" by Peter Spycher, *Die deutsche Lyrik,* ed. Benno v. Wiese (Düsseldorf, 1956), II, 191–200.

12. Spycher, p. 197.

13. G. I, 299.

14. Cf. G. I, 747.

15. Manfred Hausmann, "Unendliches Gedicht; Bemerkungen anlässlich der Lyrik Theodor Storms," *Akademie der Wissenschaften und der Literatur,* No. 2 (1962), 21–43. While Hausmann does not primarily base his findings on structural phenomena, he arrives at a similar conclusion: that of the eternal conflict behind poetry, specifically, the problem of social reality deriving from Storm's own middle-class background.

16. Cf. Clifford Bernd, "Theodor Storms Lyrik," *Nordelbingen,* 38 (1969), 104–11.

17. July 12, 1853; cf. Goldammer, I, 704.

18. G. I, 296. No attempt has been made to preserve the original meter and rhyme of the poems; they are prose translations.

19. G. I, 300.

20. G. I, 294.

21. *Der Briefwechsel zwischen Theodor Storm und Gottfried Keller,* Aufbau Verlag (Berlin, 1967), p. 50. (Dec. 27, 1879).

22. Cf. his letter of January 21, 1868, to his friend Hartmuth Brinkmann, where he explains the personal reason for this poem. G. I, 745.

23. G. I, 297. This poem is based on a poem of like title by Heinrich Heine (1851): although different in theme, it has the same tone of bitterness which characterizes Heine's satire on the Book of Matthew 13:12.

24. Cf. letter to Hartmuth Brinkmann, of Dec. 10, 1852, in *Nachgelassene Schriften,* ed. Gertrud Storm, IV: *Briefe an seine Freunde* (Braunschweig, 1917).

25. Cf. Johannes Klein, *Geschichte der deutschen Lyrik von Luther bis zum Ausgang des zweiten Weltkrieges,* 2nd edition (Wiesbaden, 1960), p. 571.

26. *Op. cit.,* p. 594.

27. "Erinnerungen an Theodor Storm," *Deutsche Revue,* XXIV. 3 (1899), p. 193 (letter dated March 3, 1874).

28. "Briefwechsel zwischen Theodor Storm und Emil Kuh," ed. Paul R. Kuh, *Westermanns Monatshefte,* LXVII (1890) pt. 1, p. 107 (September 1872). It is worth noting here that this quotation has been used with some regularity by Marxist critics to demonstrate Storm's "self-imposed limitation to a body of lyrical *Novellen* of reminiscences" (Lukács). It would seem that the emphasis here must be placed on Storm's concept of classicism rather than on an implication of a voluntary abdication from the significant issues of his own time. Cf. Georg Lukács, *Deutsche Realisten des 19. Jahrhunderts* (Berlin, 1951); Peter Goldammer, *Theodor Storm, Sämtliche Werke,* vol. I (Berlin, 1967); Fritz Böttger, *Theodor Storm in seiner Zeit* (Berlin, 1959).

29. Up to the year 1955, there had appeared seventeen hundred compositions based on lyrics by Storm. Most of them are intended for one vocalist with piano accompaniment. Cf. Hermann Fey, *Kompositionen auf Worte von Theodor Storm* (typewritten manuscript), Schleswig-Holsteinische Landesbibliothek (Kiel, 1955).

30. G. I, 192.

31. For this interpretation, cf. Peter Goldammer, "Theodor Storm und die deutsche Literaturgeschichtsschreibung," *Aufbau,* 12 (1956), 964; also, cf. G. IV, 692.

32. G. I, 113.

33. Briefwechsel, p. 22 (August 13, 1878).

34. Cf. "Einleitung," G. I, pp. 8–9.

35. *Ibid.*

36. Franz Stuckert, *Theodor Storm: Sein Leben und seine Welt* (Bremen, 1955), p. 166.

37. G. I, 184.

38. *Die literarische Formenwelt des Biedermeiers* (Giessen, 1958), pp. 14–16.

39. "Critique," 1852; G. I, 133.

40. G. I, 690.

41. G. I, 118 (stanzas 5 and 7).

42. *Op. cit.,* pp. 34–35.

43. G. I, 121. For the interpretation of this poem as an example of the frequent theme of the suffering outsider observing life but being excluded from participation, cf. Robert Pitrou, *La vie et l'oeuvre de Theodor Storm* (Paris, 1920), p. 103.

44. Gertrud Storm, *Briefe an seine Frau,* II (Braunschweig, 1915), p. 175.

45. *Ibid.,* p. 67.

46. Although there is no direct evidence of Storm's study of Feuerbach's philosophy, there are numerous parallels in the works of the two writers to justify the contention. For the paraphrase in parentheses, cf. Ludwig Feuerbach, *Gedanken über Tod und Unsterblichkeit* (Nürnberg, 1830) and for the parallels, cf. P. Westra, "Theodor Storm en Ludwig Feuerbach," *De Gids,* 113 (Amsterdam, 1950), 269–87.

47. G. I, 285.

48. Marx's criticism of Feuerbach, whom he accused of regarding human nature as static, is fully applicable to Storm. Without inferring that human nature is the exclusive product of social influences, it is fair to say that Storm considered human nature as given and unchangeable. Cf. Karl Marx, "Thesen über Feuerbach," *Marx,* Fischer, 112 (Frankfurt, 1956), 41–42.

49. G. I, 167.

50. G. I, 192. This chapter had already been written when Walter Silz' analysis of "Über die Heide" appeared late in 1970 in *Studies in German Literature of the Nineteenth and Twentieth Centuries, Festschrift for Frederic E. Coenen* (UNC Press), 1970, 105–10. It would appear that Silz and I are in essential agreement concerning the essential rhythmical and musical quality of the poem, differences concerning details notwithstanding.

51. G. I, 722.

52. *Ibid.*

53. *Op. cit.,* p. 40.

Chapter Three

(Parts of this chapter were taken from my unpublished dissertation "The Problem of Anxiety in the Works of Theodor Storm.")

1. G. I, 752.

2. *Theodor Storms Briefwechsel mit Theodor Mommsen,* ed. Erich Teitge (Weimar, 1966), p. 36.

3. "Shadows from the Void in Theodor Storm's Novellen," *The Germanic Review*, 37 (1962), p. 189.

4. *Op. cit.*, pp. 48–49.

5. G. I, 395.

6. Otto Frommel, *Neuere deutsche Dichter in ihrer religiösen Stellung* (Berlin, 1902), p. 95.

7. K. III, 211.

8. Generally, however, Storm was not prejudiced against other nations and races. However, he tended to emphasize his native culture as well as German tradition as a whole over anything not indigenous. The recorded incidences of actual prejudice toward foreignness and foreigners are extremely rare with Storm. Thus, for example, in his letter to Gottfried Keller of August 14, 1881, the anti-Semitic remarks were made in a fit of personal pique and quite in keeping with the clichés of the Bismarck era. On the whole, Storm's attitude in such matters seems to have been one of unreflected adoption of prevailing opinion or traditional belief rather than one of deliberate vilification. Cf. Storm-Keller Briefwechsel, *op. cit.*, p. 76.

9. K. III, 18.

10. K. III, 43.

11. K. VIII, 210.

12. G. I, 762.

13. André Jolles, *Einfache Formen* (Tübingen, 1930), pp. 243, 245.

14. Allen McCormick in his excellent analysis of *Hinzelmeier* comes to a similar conclusion: Cf. *Theodor Storm's Novellen. Essays on Literary Technique* (Chapel Hill, 1964), pp. 163–64.

15. These tales, therefore, are not to be regarded solely as a flight from reality. As Martini points out, they were also an attempt "to break out of the circle of psychological realism without sacrificing it." Fritz Martini, *Deutsche Literatur im Bürgerlichen Realismus, 1848–1898* (Stuttgart, 1962), p. 644.

16. G. I, 771 ff.

17. *Ibid.*, p. 774.

Chapter Four

1. For a complete typology of Storm's narrative technique and perspective, cf. Hannelore Faden, *Die Physiognomie des Erzählers bei Storm.* Unpubl. Diss. (Frankfurt a/M., 1954).

2. Franz Stuckert, "Theodor Storms novellistische Form," *Germanisch-Romanische Monatsschrift*, 27 (1939), 24–39.

3. Walter Brecht, "Storm und die Geschichte," *Deutsche Vierteljahrsschrift* III (1925), 444–62.

4. Robert M. Browning, "Association and Disassociation in Storm's

Novellen: A Study on the Meaning of the Frame," *PMLA*, LXVI (1951), 381–404.

5. K. E. Laage, *Theodor Storm und Iwan Turgenjew* (Heide, Schleswig-Holstein, 1967), pp. 38–39.

6. Clifford Bernd, *Theodor Storm's Craft of Fiction, op. cit.*

7. *Ibid.*

8. According to narrative type, to themes representative of his total oeuvre, and to various periods during his artistic career. For a further explication of the principles of selection, cf. the preface to this study.

9. K. VIII, 199–200.

10. K. I, 272.

11. K. I, 297.

12. K. I, 298.

13. K. I, 303.

14. J. Vlasimsky, "Zu Theodor Storm," *Euphorion*, XVII (1910), 359. Vlasimsky points to the Heine references in *Immensee*. On the other hand, the Gypsy girl which occurs in the novella to remind Reinhard of his commitment to Elisabeth and of his own mortality— she herself cannot tempt him—resembles in function very much Eduard Mörike's mysterious Gypsy girl Elisabeth in *Maler Nolten*.

15. K. I, 301.

16. *Nachgelassene Schriften: Briefe an seine Frau,* ed. Gertrud Storm (Braunschweig, 1915–17), p. 349.

17. "Briefwechsel zwischen Theodor Storm und Emil Kuh," ed. Paul R. Kuh, *Westermanns Monatshefte*, LXVII (1890), pt. 2, p. 265.

18. *Nachgelassene Schriften: Briefe an seine Freunde,* ed. Gertrud Storm (Braunschweig, 1915–17), pp. 53–55.

19. K. I, 299.

20. Marianne Bonwit, "Der leidende Dritte: Das Problem der Ent-sagung in bürgerlichen Romanen und Novellen, besonders bei Theodor Storm," *University of California Publications in Modern Philology,* XXXVI (1952), 104.

21. Letter to Eduard Mörike, July 6, 1865; *Briefwechsel zwischen Theodor Storm und Eduard Mörike,* ed. Hanns W. Rath (Stuttgart, 1919).

22. For this observation and explanation, cf. Faden, *ibid.,* p. 134. For the quotation, cf. K. III, 166.

23. Cf. R. M. Browning, *op. cit.,* p. 383.

24. K. VIII, 122.

25. From an unpublished letter to Wilhelm Petersen. Cf. C. Bernd, *op. cit.,* p. 57.

26. Cf. Storm's foreword to Klaus Groth's *Quickborn,* K. VIII, 118.

27. Cf. Browning, *op. cit.,* p. 398.

28. The town is not mentioned by name but its "Gelehrtenschule" (high school) is mentioned, as well as the coastal landscape, pointing to Storm's native region.

29. The actual caption reads "Aquis incuria servi submersus" (drowned through the negligence of the servant). Storm's alteration of the motif reflects his concern with the problem of heredity and other natural and social forces determining tragic fate. For the background to the inscription, cf. K. F. Boll, "Das Bonnixsche Epitaph in Drelsdorf und die Kirchenbilder in Theodor Storms 'Aquis submersus,' " *Schriften der Theodor-Storm-Gesellschaft,* 14 (1965), p. 28.

30. Cf. Storm's unpublished diary "Was der Tag giebt" (1880–83), Schleswig-Holsteinische Landesbibliothek, Kiel, p. 24 (April 8, 1883). This diary contains mostly thoughts on his already published works and on his plans and projects for others. The preface to the diary reads: "Not only of what happens each day, but also of what happened in days past and of what rises again on the present day."

31. Diary, October 1, 1880, pp. 2–3.

32. Cf. Johannes Klein, *Geschichte der deutschen Novelle von Goethe bis zur Gegenwart,* 2nd ed. (Wiesbaden, 1954), 223–70. There is, of course, the fact that in Storm's opinion the aristocracy had outlived its usefulness as a class and that the middle class should be accorded the recognition and position of political power which was its due by virtue of the already established social and economic facts in the second half of his century.

33. K. IV, 286.

34. K. IV, 287.

35. K. IV, 333.

36. K. IV, 330.

37. K. IV, 334.

38. K. IV, 335.

39. K. IV, 257. Italics mine.

40. Clifford Bernd comes to a similar conclusion when he states that the reason for the divided manuscript is that "the two copybooks . . . most likely will become detached from one another after the passing of time." *Op. cit.,* p. 22.

41. The narrator of this novella refers to himself as a writer and dispassionate observer of the human scene, driven by "an insatiable anthropological appetite." The poor musician, on the other hand, is endowed with traits which resemble closely Grillparzer's own, both as a human being and an artist. Hence, the author appears divided into spectator and participant.

42. K. V, 229.

43. K. V, 230.

44. K. V, 271.

45. Benno von Wiese makes the same point for all of Storm's reminiscent tales: "The Stormian 'frame of reminiscence' does not create an objective distance toward that which is represented, but a subjective proximity which enables the narrator to report from a narrative perspective which is entirely personal." *Novelle*. Stuttgart: Metzler, 1964, p. 70.

46. K. VI, 52.

47. *Ibid.*

48. K. VI, 56.

49. K. VI, 74.

50. K. VI, 77.

51. K. VI, 113.

52. K. VI, 125.

53. Benno von Wiese, *Die deutsche Novelle von Goethe bis Kafka,* vol. II (Düsseldorf, 1964), p. 223 (from an unpublished letter).

54. *Ibid.*, p. 228.

55. K. VI, 123 f.

56. K. VI, 121.

57. Benno von Wiese asserts that the opposite is true. "Not the conciliatory harmonization of dissonances makes Storm convincing today, but the sudden rift of irreconcilable antinomies which exist between atmosphere and reality." *Ibid.*, pp. 220 f.

58. *Ibid.*, p. 234.

59. Jost Hermand, *Die literarische Formenwelt des Biedermeiers,* p. 90.

60. *Op. cit.* The entries concerning Grieshuus in his unpublished diary relate to notes on the historical background to Grieshuus.

61. Cf. Johannes Klein, *op. cit.*, pp. 233–70.

62. *Briefwechsel, op. cit.*, September 13, 1883, p. 123. Paul Heyse's Falcon Theory stipulates that a *Novelle* should have a surprising turning point like the killing of the falcon in Boccaccio's *Decamerone*.

63. Franz Stuckert, *op. cit.*, p. 373.

64. K. VI, 207.

65. K. VI, 218.

66. K. VI, 241.

67. K. VI, 289.

68. K. VI, 247.

69. K. VI, 262.

70. K. VI, 249; 293.

71. K. VI, 263.

72. K. VI, 264.

73. Cf. Franz Stuckert, *op. cit.*, p. 377.

74. K. VI, 198.

75. K. VI, 241; 259 f.

76. Paul Böckmann, in an important essay, makes similar observations concerning this novella as well as Storm's production as a whole: "Storm's realism . . . consists of reminiscences through which reality can be related as experienced reality." Böckmann confirms our own thesis of Storm's basic subjectivity by analyzing the similarities between Storm's and Fontane's theories and writings. Fontane praised Storm's basic honesty of form in his novellas which he called a specific Stormian quality: "through his subjectively recalled world does Storm reveal his own relationship to reality. Even his provincialism which, according to Fontane, pervades his entire oeuvre is justified and becomes meaningful as the preservation of a subjectivity which finds itself limited by its own level of experience and which is realized within these limits without being able or even wanting to mythologize or canonize the homeland." Needless to add, that Böckmann's analysis contravenes Thomas Mann's interpretation of Fontane's dictum about Storm's Husum-oriented provincialism in his famous essay on Storm. According to Böckmann, Fontane actually meant to characterize thereby Storm's quality as a writer which could assert itself best within the limitations of the familiar, of homeland and family. Cf. "Theodor Storm und Fontane; Ein Beitrag zur Funktion der Erinnerung in Storms Erzählkunst," *Schriften der Theodor-Storm-Gesellschaft,* 17 (1968), pp. 92; 88.

77. Unpublished letter of June 8, 1866; Landesbibliothek Schleswig-Holstein.

78. K. VII, 2.

79. *Briefe an seine Freunde, op. cit.,* pp. 209–11.

80. K. VII, 72.

81. K. VII, pp. 14, 39, 42.

82. K. VII, 39.

83. G. IV, 643.

84. G. IV, 644.

85. K. VII, 135.

86. K. VII, 166.

87. K. VII, 191.

88. On this point, cf. Hannelore Faden, *op. cit.,* pp. 115–17. Faden, quite rightly, points out that the role of the narrator as a friendly and helpful intelligence in the forester's house does not agree with his sudden revelation that the entire tale was pure fiction, the product of his visionary gift.

89. K. VII, 164.

90. K. VII, 191.

91. K. VII, 179.

92. Cf. Chapter 3, note 4 of this study.

93. August 29, 1886. *Heyse-Storm Briefwechsel.* Georg Plotke, ed. 2 vols. (München, 1918).

94. K. VII, 252.

95. K. VII, 253 f.

96. K. VII, 256.

97. K. VII, 297.

98. Walter Silz, "Theodor Storm: Der Schimmelreiter," *Realism and Reality* (Chapel Hill, 1962), pp. 122 ff.

99. Volker Knüfermann, *Realismus. Untersuchungen zur sprachlichen Wirklichkeit der Novellen "Im Nachbarhause links," "Hans und Heinz Kirch," und "Der Schimmelreiter" von Theodor Storm.* Diss. (unpubl.), Münster, 1967, p. 99.

100. *Ibid.,* October 20, 1887.

101. *Ibid.,* p. 118.

102. K. VII, 264.

103. Cf. Knüfermann, *op. cit.,* p. 118.

104. On this point, cf. Walter Silz, *op. cit.,* pp. 121 f. and Ernst Loeb, "Faust ohne Transzendenz: Theodor Storms *Schimmelreiter,*" *Studies in Germanic Languages and Literatures. In Memory of Fred O. Nolte.* (St. Louis, Mo., 1963), 121–32.

105. K. VII, 377.

106. Silz, *op. cit.,* p. 130.

107. K. VII, 323.

108. *Ibid.,* p. 125.

109. Knüfermann, *op. cit.,* pp. 115 ff.

110. K. VII, 301.

111. For these points cf. Silz, *op. cit.,* p. 125.

112. K. VII, 299.

113. K. VII, 346.

114. K. VII, 372 f.

115. Jost Hermand, "Hauke Haien, Kritik oder Ideal des gründerzeitlichen Übermenschen?", *Wirkendes Wort,* 15 (1965), 40–50.

116. *Ibid.,* p. 120.

Chapter Five

1. For a fairly thorough assessment by scholars from many parts of the world of Storm's significance in the history of literature today, cf. *Schriften der Theodor-Storm-Gesellschaft,* 17 (1967), commemorating Storm's 150th birthday.

2. Paul Böckmann, "Theodor Storm und Fontane," *op. cit.,* pp. 87 f.

3. Theodor Fontane, *Sämtliche Werke,* Kurt Schreinert, ed. vol. XXI, I (München, 1963), p. 498.

4. *Storm's Craft of Fiction,* cf. Bernd, *op. cit.*

5. About his Christmas idyl, the vignette *Unter dem Tannenbaum* (*Under the Christmas Tree*) and in response to some criticism by his friend Hartmuth Brinkmann about its remoteness from any great issue, Storm wrote: "My Christmas idyl, I believe, was a very fortunate choice and was written with great warmth. Your criticism is unjustified; after all, this concerns my homeland and my sympathy for it. I am willing to admit that it is subordinate to the greater sentiment for one's country—just as the latter may be second to the sentiment of world citizenship; but that cannot detract from its wholly human significance." April 4, 1863, *op. cit.*

6. Erich Auerbach, *Mimesis. Dargestellte Wirklichkeit in der abendländischen Literatur.* Bern, 1946. Georg Lukács, *Deutsche Realisten des 19. Jahrhunderts.* Berlin, 1951. Robert Minder, *Der Dichter in der Gesellschaft.* Frankfurt a/M, 1966.

7. "Gedichtete Perspektiven in Storms Erzählkunst," *Schriften der Theodor-Storm-Gesellschaft,* 17 (1967), p. 26.

Selected Bibliography

a) The most important editions of Storm's works and letters:

Sämtliche Werke. Ed. Elbert Köster, 8 vols. Leipzig: Insel Verlag, 1919–20. This has been the standard edition.

Sämtliche Werke. Ed. Peter Goldammer, 2nd ed., 4 vols. Berlin: Aufbau Verlag, 1967. This edition is based on the standard Köster edition but contains much updated material in the notes as well as poems and letters which had come to light since Köster's publication.

Nachgelassene Schriften. Ed. Gertrud Storm, 4 vols. Braunschweig: Westermann Verlag, 1915–17. These letters, edited by his daughter, concern those to his fiancée, his wife, his children, and his friends Hartmuth Brinkmann and Wilhelm Petersen. Filial love prompted Gertrud to present her father's memory to the world in as favorable a light as possible; hence this edition is in many ways unreliable. As yet, however, it remains the standard edition.

Der Briefwechsel zwischen Theodor Storm und Gottfried Keller. Ed. Peter Goldammer, 2nd ed., Berlin: Aufbau Verlag, 1967.

Briefwechsel zwischen Theodor Storm und Eduard Mörike. Ed. Hanns Wolfgang Rath. Stuttgart: Hoffmann, 1919.

Theodor Storm–Paul Heyse, Briefwechsel. Ed. Clifford Bernd, 2 vols. Berlin: Erich Schmidt, 1969–70. The third volume of this important and extensive correspondence is to be published in 1972.

b) Bibliographies:

Theodor Storm Bibliographie. Ed. Hans-Erich Teitge. Berlin: Deutsche Staatsbibliothek, 1967. This bibliography supersedes the previous compilations by Wooley, Gebauer, and Bernd.

c) Translations:

Immensee or the Old Man's Reverie. Trans. Helene Clark. Münster: Brunn Verlag, 1863. This translation was done with Storm's knowledge and approval. (The first translation of *Immensee* had the subtitle *A Dream of Youth* and appeared in Colburn's *New*

Monthly Magazine and Literary Journal in 1858.) Since then, it has been translated into English eleven times, the most recent being:

Immensee. Trans. Ronald Taylor. London: Calder & Boyars, 1966.
The Little Stepmother. Trans. B. Q. Morgan. *Curator Carsten.* Trans. Frieda Voigt. New York: Ungar; London: Calder, 1956.
Aquis submersus. Trans. James Millar. London: Gowans & Gray, 1910.
Eekenhof. Trans. James Millar. London: Gowans & Gray, 1908.
Renate. Trans. James Millar. London: Gowans & Gray, 1909.
The Senator's Sons. Trans. E. M. Huggard. London: Harrap, 1947.
A Festival at Haderslevhuus. Trans. James Millar. London: Gowans & Gray, 1909.
A Chapter in the History of Grieshuus. Trans. James Millar. London: Gowans & Gray, 1908.
The Rider on the White Horse and Selected Stories. Trans. James Wright. New York: New American Library, 1964.

Only a few of Storm's poems have been translated into English:
"Oktoberlied." Trans. Carlyle F. MacIntyre. Los Angeles: Ward Ritchie Press, 1945.
The Penguin Book of German Verse. Ed. Leonard Forster. Penguin Books, D. 36, 1959. It contains a small number of Storm's poems in prose translation by Forster on pp. 358–63.

SECONDARY SOURCES

ALT, TILO. "Das Phänomen der Erschütterung bei Theodor Storm," *Schriften der Theodor-Storm-Gesellschaft,* XV (1966), 40–46. Similar to our argument that Storm's oeuvre must be regarded under the aspect of a tragic view of life, the article traces the phenomenon of tragic emotion in his works.

BERND, CLIFFORD. *Theodor Storm's Craft of Fiction.* 2nd ed. Chapel Hill: University of North Carolina Press, 1966. An important book by one of the foremost Storm scholars in America. The study concerns a model structural analysis of Storm's *In St. Jürgen* and *Aquis submersus.* The Appendix informs about the state of Storm scholarship, location of manuscripts, and bibliography. The appendix is indispensable to the serious Storm scholar.

BONWIT, MARIANNE. "Der leidende Dritte: Das Problem der Entsagung in bürgerlichen Romanen und Novellen, besonders bei Theodor Storm," *University of California Publications in Modern Philology,* XXXVI (1952), 91–112. The austere concept of marriage and society conflicts with the desires and rights of the individual and conflicts arise; certain patterns emerge and are traced in this article concerning Storm's novellas.

BOTZONG, HERTHA. *Wesen und Wert von Storms Märchendichtung.* München: Salsesianische Offizin, 1935.

BRECHT, WALTHER. "Storm und die Geschichte," *Deutsche Viertel-jahrsschrift für Literaturwissenschaft und Geistesgeschichte,* III (1925), 444–62. This article seeks to determine Storm's concept of history, particularly with regard to the chronicle novellas.

BROWNING, ROBERT. "Association and Disassociation in Storm's Novellen: A Study on the Meaning of the Frame," *Publications of the Modern Language Association of America,* LXVI (1951), 381–404.

FEISE, ERNST. *Xenion: Themes, Forms, and Ideas in German Literature.* Baltimore, Maryland, 1950. Contains an important analysis of *Aquis submersus.*

GOLDAMMER, PETER. *Theodor Storm: Eine Einführung in Leben und Werk.* Leipzig: Philipp Reclam, 1966. An analysis of Storm's life and works from the Marxist point of view.

HERMAND, JOST. "Hauke Haien: Kritik oder Ideal des gründerzeitlichen Übermenschen?" *Wirkendes Wort,* XV (1965), 40–50. An important article discussing the main character of *Schimmelreiter* in the light of the "heroic" age of Bismarck's Germany.

JENNINGS, LEE. "Shadows from the Void in Theodor Storm's Novellen," *The Germanic Review,* XXXVII (1962), 174–89. The essay deals with the element of the supernatural in Storm's oeuvre.

LAAGE, KARL ERNST. *Theodor Storm und Iwan Turgenjew: Persönliche Beziehungen und Literarische Einflüsse, Briefe, Bilder.* Heide: Westholsteinische Verlaganstalt Boyens & Co., 1967. Aside from the discussion of the relationship of the two poets, the volume reproduces the entire correspondence between these men.

LOEB, ERNST. "Faust ohne Transzendenz: Theodor Storms Schimmelreiter," *Studies in Germanic Languages and Literatures.* St. Louis: Washington University Press, 1963, 121–32. Traces the parallels and differences between the striving of Goethe's Faust, part II and Hauke Haien's quest for superiority over nature.

MANN, THOMAS. *Adel des Geistes.* Stockholm: S. Fischer, 1955. A confessional essay by the writer Thomas Mann discussing the formative influence Storm had on Mann's concept of German literature.

McCORMICK, ALLEN. *Theodor Storm's Novellen: Essays on Literary Technique.* Chapel Hill: University of North Carolina Press, 1964.

PROCKSCH, AUGUST. "Der Wortschatz Theodor Storms," *Germanisch-Romanische Monatsschrift,* VI (1914), 532–62. The article discusses Storm's poetic vocabulary in statistical detail and is indispensable to the scholar interested in Storm's literary style.

Schriften der Theodor-Storm-Gesellschaft (1952–   ). The annual publication of the Storm Society in Husum. Since its inception twenty issues have appeared. The issues contain much documentary and manuscript material, previously unpublished, as well as important essays dealing with all manner of aspects of Storm's literary work. This periodical is indispensable to the scholar as well as to the interested layman.

SCHUMANN, WILLY. *The Technique of Characterization in the Late Novellas of Theodor Storm*. Dissertation: Columbia University. New York, 1959.

————. "Theodor Storm und Thomas Mann. Gemeinsames und Unterschiedliches," *Schriften der Theodor-Storm-Gesellschaft*, XIII (1964), 28–44.

SILZ, WALTER. "Theodor Storm's Schimmelreiter," *Publications of the Modern Language Association of America*, LXI (1946), 762–83. A close analysis of Storm's masterpiece.

————. "Theodor Storm: Three Poems," *The Germanic Review*, 42 (1967), 293–300. An analysis of Storm's "Die Stadt," "Oktoberlied," "Juli."

————. "Theodor Storm's *Über die Heide*," *Festschrift for Frederic E. Coenen*. Chapel Hill: University of North Carolina Press, 1970; pp. 105–10. The only discussion of this well-known poem in English.

STUCKERT, FRANZ. *Theodor Storm: Sein Leben und seine Welt*. Bremen, 1955. The standard biography in German.

WEDBERG, LLOYD. *The Theme of Loneliness in Theodor Storm's Novellen*. The Hague: Mouton & Co., 1964.

WIESE, BENNO v. *Die deutsche Novelle von Goethe bis Kafka*, vol. II. Düsseldorf: Bagel, 1964. It contains a close analysis of Storm's *Hans und Heinz Kirch*. Von Wiese also seeks to challenge the primacy of *Der Schimmelreiter* in Storm's oeuvre.

WOOLEY, ELMER. *Studies in Theodor Storm*. Bloomington: Indiana University Press, 1943. Includes a bibliography and several essays dealing with various aspects of Storm's works.

————. *Theodor Storm's World in Pictures*. Bloomington: Indiana University Press, 1954. Contains 300 pictures and photographs of people and places in Storm's life.

Index